THE ANATOMY OF

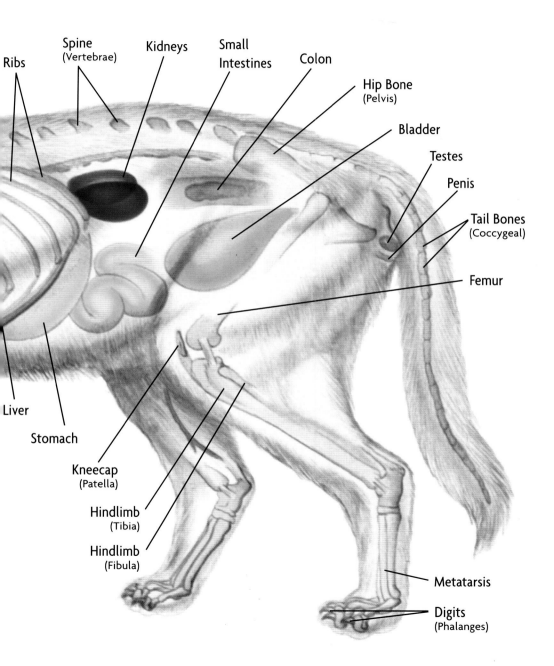

Ribs

Spine
(Vertebrae)

Kidneys

Small
Intestines

Colon

Hip Bone
(Pelvis)

Bladder

Testes

Penis

Tail Bones
(Coccygeal)

Femur

Liver

Stomach

Kneecap
(Patella)

Hindlimb
(Tibia)

Hindlimb
(Fibula)

Metatarsis

Digits
(Phalanges)

Russian Blue Cat

By Dennis Kelsey-Wood

CONTENTS

PUBLISHED IN THE UNITED KINGDOM BY:

INTERPET
P U B L I S H I N G

Vincent Lane, Dorking   Surrey RH4 3YX   England

ISBN 1-84286-050-X

PHOTO CREDITS
Photography by Isabelle Francais and Alan Robinson
with additional photographs by Cat Fanciers Association,
Carolina Biological Supply, Fleabusters Rx for Fleas, James R Hayden, RBP,
Interpet, Dwight R Kuhn, Dr Dennis Kunkel, Mikki Pet Products,
Phototake, Jean Claude Revy, and WB Saunders Company.

The publisher wishes to thank all of the owners of the cats featured in
this book, including Wendy Lund and the Kurpienkos.

History of the

RUSSIAN BLUE CAT

With an early history that has been lost in the midst of theories, half-truths, fanciful notions and reality, the Russian Blue is one of only a few breeds that predate the beginnings of the cat fancy as an organised hobby. More so than with a number of its pre-cat-fancy contemporaries, it can at times be impossible to establish exactly what occurred before the point in the breed's history where theory gives way to verifiable documentation.

BLUE CATS

There are at this time four cats recognised as having a long history as blue breeds. These are the British Blue, the Chartreuse of France, the Korat of Thailand and, our subject, the Russian Blue. All other blue cats merely are varieties of other breeds. This is actually true of the British Blue, but its importance as a blue cat is historical.

In the earliest years of the cat fancy, other blues were evident. These included the Spanish, the Maltese, the Icelandic and the American Blue. While each of the surviving European blues is

claimed by their devotees to have been the ancestor of the other European breeds, there is no evidence to substantiate such claims.

Blue cats have been present in Europe and Asia for many centuries and it would be quite impossible to say from where they originated. Nor should it be assumed that a single original source of blue was necessarily the case. It is quite possible that the causal mutation of the blue (and of longhair) has appeared numerous times and in different parts of the world.

So, in the years prior to the first cat show, there existed in England a number of blue cats.

The concept of breed versus variety can be quite confusing in the cat world. It was once felt that blue cats, regardless of origin, were varieties of the British Shorthair, shown here, rather than distinct cat breeds.

These had arrived from various countries—taken there by returning or visiting travellers. There was also a quite large indigenous population of blue cats. Such was the blue cat's situation as the cat fancy as an organised hobby was to emerge.

It is thought that the first Russian Blues, then called Archangel Cats, had arrived in Britain about 1860 from Archangel (Arkhangelsk). This is a port situated near the mouth of the Dwina River on the White Sea, which exits into the Arctic Ocean in northern Russia. It was Russia's only port until 1703, when St. Petersburg was founded on the Baltic Sea.

THE FIRST CAT SHOW
On the Thursday, 13 July 1871, at the Crystal Palace, Sydenham,

London, the world's first multi-breed cat show was staged. Its organiser was Harrison Weir, a noted artist, naturalist and expert on poultry. The show proved a great success, so much so that other shows followed in Britain and throughout the world. Cat clubs and registration bodies were created and the cat fancy was underway.

The breed standards prepared by Harrison Weir were so good that they provided the model for those used to this very day. At that first show, blue cats were exhibited, but we know little about these.

BREED OR VARIETY?
In the early years of the cat fancy, the concept of what constituted a breed was very different than that of today. Although breeds such as the Archangel (which was soon renamed the Russian Cat or Russian Blue) and the Chartreuse initially were given names based on their believed countries of origin, this simple nomenclature soon changed.

A newer view was closer to the reality of the situation. Weir believed (correctly, as it turned out) that blue cats were merely light varieties of the black cat, a view he based on the fact that some top winners were produced from non-blue parents. These, in turn, were merely varieties of the English shorthaired cat, the name then used for the British Shorthair.

He also thought that all other names applied to blue cats (Chartreuse, Spanish, *et al*) were merely alternative names for the same cat.

Weir, writing on blue cats, stated that he saw no distinction in form, temperament or habit between British cats and those claimed to be foreign. But he then goes on to say, 'I feel bound, however, to admit that those that came from Archangel were of a deeper, purer tint than the English cross-breeds…I find that they had larger ears and eyes, and were larger and longer in the head and legs, also the coat or fur was

MRS CAREW-COX
In spite of the prevalent trend of that time against the Russian Blue, one breeder who stoically worked with the breed in the last years of the 19th century, and continued into the new one, was Mrs Carew-Cox. Among her cats were Olga (imported 1893) and Fashoda (1896).

When mated to King Vladimir, Olga produced a well-known stud called Bayard, who was born in 1898. In that same year, Mrs Carew-Cox purchased Dwina (named for the Russian river), whose origins were unknown. In 1901, Yula was imported. It is said that these various imports came from Archangel, though some reports suggest that they may have been from Norway.

excessively short, rather inclined to woolliness, but bright and glossy, the hair inside the ears being shorter than is usual in the English cat.'

The foregoing extract was taken from Weir's book *Our Cats and All About Them*. This was originally published in 1889 and revised in 1892. The colour description would match that of the present-day English type of Russian Blue, as would the face and eye shape, based on his accompanying drawing of the Archangel Blue Cat. In contrast, his comment regarding the excessively short coat would not match present-day requirements, nor would the eye colour or today's need for upright position of the ears in British and European Russian Blues.

In the standard for the Blue Shorthair given in Weir's book, it is required that the eyes be large, round and full. The fur was required to be short, of even length, smooth, silky and glossy— and lying close to the body. There is no mention of the woolliness he had ascribed to the Archangel Cat earlier in the book. The legs were required to be of medium length and the body narrow, long and graceful, with a rather long and slender neck.

BREED TYPES MERGED

The first cat show generated an increased awareness of the feline hobby, which created a demand for pure-bred kittens as well as cats of exhibition potential. Felines of Russian, Spanish, Chartreuse and other origins would be seen only rarely.

These would have been mated indiscriminately to each other. The Russian cat appears to be the only one of the blues that had a distinct type when compared to the other 'cross-breed' blues, as Weir, by 1889, called them. In this situation, it would not take too long for the Russian type to lose any individuality that it may originally have had.

Surprisingly, although the coat of the Russian Blue was, by the turn of the century, recognised as being different to that of other types, it was still felt that it was not a separate breed. As a consequence, it was placed with the English shorthairs for exhibition purposes. This did not favour its retention of type. Cats with the Russian-type fur were penalised for having incorrect coat texture when compared against the standard, which of course was based on the English-type coat!

THE BREED IN DECLINE

Although the Russian Blue was given its own show class in 1912, this lasted but a few years. The Russian Revolution of 1917 clearly influenced matters in a negative manner. As a consequence, the use of the name 'Russian' was dropped

While white and black colour varieties of the Russian Blue have been recognised by Britain's Governing Council of the Cat Fancy (GCCF), the only colour accepted in the US is the original blue, shown here.

in that year, and the breed was merged with the Foreign Blue.

The 'Foreign' group of cats was created in order to house breeds such as the Siamese. The self-blue Siamese (the Oriental Blue of today) was the basis of the Foreign Blue, so the sort of confusion that reigned will be appreciated. The Siamese self-blue in those days looked rather similar to the Russian and was green-eyed.

It was sometime around the late 1920s/early 1930s that the green eye colour of the Russian is seen, and it appears in the standard of about 1933. It must be assumed that it was transferred from a breed such as the British Silver Tabby or the Siamese-based Foreign Blue.

Interestingly, in 1912, you could purchase a Russian Blue for twelve shillings and six pence. That was quite a bit of cash for the average person, but was inexpensive compared to the two pounds two and six pence required to purchase an Abyssinian. The Aby was thus 340% more costly!

PIONEER BREEDERS
The fortunes of the Russian Blue (Foreign Blue) steadily deteriorated throughout the decades that followed the 1920s, when only a handful of breeders kept it alive. The most notable prefix seen during the 1920s was Coryton, though Cleave also appears in pedigrees. In the following decade,

Miss Pelly, whose cattery was called Theydon, was the major force in the breed.

In 1943, another lady became involved with the breed. This was Miss M Rochford, whose Dunloe prefix was to become arguably the most famous and influential in the history of the breed. By this period, the prefixes of a few breeders in other countries were gaining fame. These included Bellahoj, Elsdorff and Finlandia (Denmark), Hoeller (USA) and Olsenburg (Sweden).

HYBRIDISATION
It is clear that the Russian Blue already had been hybridised from its earliest days, but in the 1940s, and until at least the late 1960s, hybridisation became essential for the breed's survival. Miss Rochford outcrossed to the British Blue and

A NATURAL BREED
The Russian Blue is often described as being a 'natural' breed. This is a very loose term that may have applied originally to just a very few breeds, though in almost all instances it cannot be applied to them today. Like so many other long-established 'natural' breeds, the Russian Blue (and its white, black and longhaired forms) is actually the consequence of a mutation (its colour/hair length) and has been hybridised on numerous occasions during its development.

Vivid green is the only accepted eye colour for the adult Russian Blue, a point upon which all standards world-wide agree.

to the bluepoint Siamese. This was essential because the Russian gene pool was becoming very small.

Other breeders also used the Siamese. In the quest to create the Havana, a self-chocolate Siamese, Armitage Hargreaves of the Laurentide cattery used the Russian Blue in the early 1950s. In the process, she hoped to improve the Russian Blue's conformation.

Blue offspring from her programme were in fact registered as Russian Blues. The Russian Blue was also crossed to other breeds, including the Cornish Rex in the 1960s as part of that breed's development programme, and the Persian, possibly to improve coat density. However, it was the Siamese that was the most frequently used breed.

These numerous Siamese outcrosses were to prove very significant to the breed's future development. During this period, the Russian Blue did regain its name again in Britain. It was changed from Foreign Blue to Russian Blue in 1948, though it had still been listed in the 1939 studbook as Russian Blue.

In 1951, the Russian Blue Cat Club was formed. On 4 July 1952, the breed's standard was revised to reflect the change in its type created by the Siamese. This outcross, however, did nothing for the famed coat of the Russian, which was now required to be 'short, close-lying with a distinct

RUSSIAN BLACK AND RUSSIAN WHITE

The Russian Black and the Russian White varieties gained recognition with the Governing Council of the Cat Fancy (GCCF) during the 1980s and are also varieties of the Russian in Australia and New Zealand, but these colours have made little progress. They are not accepted as breed varieties in America. I must confess, as beautiful as these are, I am somewhat doubtful as to their place alongside the Russian Blue breed.

It can be argued that there have been blacks and whites (and reds and patterned varieties) turning up in litters since the very earliest of days. However, these were purely a consequence of needed outcrossing, not the purpose of it. While no cat breed is immutable, the Russian Blue's entire reason for becoming a breed was, before all else, its colour. When this is removed, and other colours added, its historical uniqueness goes with it.

The whole question of new colours and patterns in breeds, and the creation of new breeds, is highly complex. The cat fancy always needs to embrace progressive ideas, but it should also ensure that old traditional breeds do not get trampled in the process. This will undermine the credibility of our lovely hobby. Unfortunately, these matters will never be resolved to the satisfaction of all parties.

The Russian Blue was used in the development of this breed, the Cornish Rex.

The Siamese, shown here, was used at different stages of the Russian Blue's development and revitalisation.

sheen.' The silvery sheen was not a requirement. These numerous changes had a negative effect on the breed, and in 1963 the breed club was closed.

THE BREED'S REVIVAL

The Shorthaired Cat Society was instrumental in keeping Russian Blue breeders together, and, as a consequence, the breed standard of 1939 was reintroduced. In 1965, the standard was revised and it specified that the Siamese type was undesirable.

In spite of the problems, the nucleus of active breeders was making progress in exports. Russian Blues were sent to Scandinavia, where the breed was, and remains, highly regarded. British stock also was sent to both Australia and America, where the Russian was the centre of great interest. The export of stock from Scandinavia to America was also vital in developing the breed in that country.

In 1968, the breed's gene pool was still low and valuable imports

The Balinese, a longhaired breed based on the Siamese's conformation.

The Somali, a longhaired Abyssinian.

came from Denmark and Sweden. In that same year, the Russian Blue Association (now Russian Blue Breeders Association) was formed by Miss Laugher of the well-known Jennymay cattery.

Throughout the 1970s to the present day, the fortunes of the Russian Blue have been better. Efforts to return the breed type, and especially its coat, to what it was in the early years of the breed have been successful. However, this said, there are still differences in the face and general conformation of the breed in different countries, and in breeding lines, due to the mixed ancestry of former years.

THE NEBELUNG (RUSSIAN BLUE LONGHAIR)

The merit of Nebelung is not on historical grounds—though it would qualify on that basis. Rather, it is because the breed does not challenge the standing and uniqueness of the Russian Blue. Indeed, it complements it and creates a new and logical breed without creating tidal waves in the process.

The Nebelung compares with the Somali (longhaired

Abyssinian), the Balinese (longhaired Siamese), the Tiffanie (longhaired Burmese), the British Angora (longhaired Oriental) and the Exotic (shorthaired Persian). Who would deny that each of these delightful breeds have done nothing but enhance the range of cat breeds to the benefit of the cat fancy as a whole?

Developing their own gene pool, but one based on the Russian Blue's conformation and initial gene input, the Nebelung would create an ideal outcross breed should this ever be needed again by the Russian Blue. It would minimise the potential for a repetition of past problems that always followed the use of unrelated outcrosses.

ORIGINAL RUSSIAN LONGHAIRS
Nebelung breeders often state that longhaired Russian cats were present from the first cat shows in Britain. This is true, but it would be misleading to imply by reference to the first shows that these were Russian Blue longhairs, or that they compared in any way with the Nebelung.

The Russian Longhairs appearing in the early shows were tabby, though the occasional black was also seen. Based on Weir's description of 1889, they were similar to the British Wild Cat (*Felis sylvestris*). The breed, like the Angora, was absorbed into the Persian, and disappeared from the cat fancy almost as soon as it arrived. With this introduction stated, we can now look at the Nebelung.

I am indebted to Cora E Cobb (Nebelheim cattery), the breed's founder, of Denver, Colorado, USA, for information on this most attractive breed. The name 'Nebelung' is derived from 'Nibelungenlied,' a very old German epic poem about a mythical supernatural race. In Europe the breed is sometimes called the 'Nibelung.'

The Chartreux, France's contribution to the blue cat breeds.

A brown classic tabby Exotic Shorthair, a shorthaired Persian.

NEBELUNG HISTORY

The breed's history commenced in 1983 when a black female moggie called Terri, owned by John Hruza, was mated with a black Turkish-Angora-type male. In the resulting litter of that year was a shorthaired female, Elsa, who was carrying the gene for both longhair and dilution. In due course, she mated with a blue shorthair thought to be a Russian Blue. This was also carrying the gene for longhair.

In the litter, born on 24 August 1984, was a longhaired blue male, Siegfried. A second litter, on 25 January 1985, produced Brunhilde, another blue longhair. These were the founding cats of the breed and were acquired by Cora Cobb in 1985.

EARLY PROBLEMS

Cora had not been involved in the cat fancy prior to owning Sig and Brun. In 1987, she exhibited a female called Schatzi (out of Sig and Brun) and was surprised to find that the concept of a longhaired Russian Blue did not go down well with Russian Blue breeders. This made it very difficult to obtain suitable studs. Initially she did so only by agreeing that the stud's name would remain anonymous.

However, Cora persevered and the breed gained recognition with The International Cat Association (TICA) in 1987 as a new breed. It was based on the standard of the Russian Blue, but with a long coat.

Dianna Zinn (Pyskitt) was the

first Russian Blue breeder to openly get involved with the Nebelung programme. Others were interested, but held back because they felt this might negatively affect their relationship with other breeders. This is not an uncommon happening with new breeds based on long-established breeds. Each of the breeds discussed earlier were subject to debate (also sadly to animosity) during their developmental years.

PRESENT AND FUTURE
The Nebelung obtained recognition with the Cat Fanciers Federation (CFF) in 1990 and championship status in the same year with the Traditional Cat Association (TCA). A major milestone occurred in 1997 when it gained championship status with TICA. At this time, the breed is still very much in the rare breeds category but is already seen in Spain, Germany, France and Russia. A number of individuals have also now become champions in America.

There are already notable cats

who are stamping their quality on the breed. Ch Winter Day Georgin of Nebelheim (male) was bred by Natasha Stolyarovi (Winter Day) and imported by Cora Cobb from Russia. Georgin was bred directly from champion Russian Blue lines carrying the longhair gene. Ch Pyskitts Silver Streak of Romani, a female Best of Breed (new breeds) winner in St. Petersburg, Russia, was bred by Dianna Zinn and Cora Cobb. Grand Ch Psykitts Give Me Kissy (female) was bred by Dianna Zinn.

Apart from the catteries already mentioned, those of Vicki Brewer (HanoHano), Louise D Safron (Paradigm), Cassie Kanick (BlueMist), Barbara Powers (Galena) and John Hruza (Romani) are other catteries now building a growing and excellent reputation for this breed. Their prefixes will no doubt be credited in the historic annals of the breed.

Like each of the other equivalent semi-longhaired breeds (which is also true of the long-established Turkish Angora and Van breeds), the Nebelung, unfortunately, will probably never attain undue popularity in the immediate coming years. But it is an elegant and worthy addition to the ranks of our domestic felines. It offers an opportunity, and challenge, to British and European breeders as well as to those in other countries who may be seeking to add a very beautiful breed to their catteries.

The Russian Blue's distinct blue coat, striking green eyes and elegant conformation are but a few of the traits that attract admirers to the breed.

Say hello to the Russian Blue, a most unique and magnificent breed of cat.

Portrait of the

RUSSIAN BLUE CAT

Of elegant classic foreign type, the Russian Blue is neither unduly stocky nor anything near as svelte as breeds like the Siamese and the Oriental Shorthair. The breed is famed not only for its blue coat colour but also for the quality of its coat, which must be felt to be fully appreciated.

The White and the Black Russian Shorthairs, as well as the Nebelung (longhaired Russian Blue), where these are accepted breeds, are judged against the same standard as the Russian Blue, with appropriate changes in reference to the colour or hair length. The Russian Blue is normally found within the weight range of 3.2–4.1 kgs (7–9 lbs) in males and 2.3–3.5 kgs (5–7.5 lbs) in females. Of course, there will always be cats that are rather heavier than the upper limits given. The Nebelung tends to be slightly heavier than its shorthaired cousin.

OFFICIAL BREED STANDARD

A breed standard is a written document that acts as a guide to what a quality example of any specific breed should look like. It usually is drafted by a breed's first national club, a group of breeders or, in some instances (as in the Nebelung), by a breed's founder. This document is then presented to a feline registry for its consideration and adoption. If the standard meets the requirements of that registry, it is then accepted and given breed status.

Every developed country has one or more feline registries, but it does not follow that each of these registries will give a breed recognition. In some instances, it is because the breed, though recognised elsewhere, does not meet a registry's particular requirements. It also may be because there are insufficient numbers of that breed to meet the numerical requirements.

The standard, once adopted, becomes the yardstick against which breeders and judges alike assess the quality in any individual cat of that breed. In cat shows, the judge compares one cat

The Russian Blue's coat is special in both colour and texture. It is dense, soft and wonderful to touch.

against another based on the judge's interpretation of the standard and how closely each cat conforms to the standard. The standard is thus of paramount importance within the cat fancy.

DIFFERENCES AMONG STANDARDS

The standards of a given registry, while being essentially similar to those of other associations, will never be duplicates. At an international level, standards may show many more differences than those of associations within the same country. The reason this happens is because, over a span of time, the preferences for certain breed features in one country may differ from those in others.

With quarantine barriers becoming less of a problem as a consequence of Pet Passports in Europe, it is likely that breed 'type' will, in the coming years, become more uniform across more countries. Presently, distinctions between many breeds in America and those in the rest of the world are evident, this being true of the Russian Blue.

LIMITATIONS OF THE STANDARD

A breed's standard can never be more than a guide; it can never be a definitive description. No two cats are ever exactly the same, thus the standard must allow for this fact. As a consequence, many terms used in a standard are relative and thus, to the novice,

are rather vague.

For example, terms such as long, short, medium, rather wide, in proportion to, modified wedge or graceful only have meaning if

BREED POPULARITY

The Russian Blue has never been an highly popular breed and, as such, is very much a connoisseur's cat. Many in the breed prefer that it remains that way. This said, the downside of being a numerically small breed does present problems.

Maintaining a sound gene pool is always a delicate balancing act, which can at times necessitate outcrossing. This tends to set a breed back for a while. Presently, the Russian Blue maintains a steady band of dedicated enthusiasts around the world, but a number of new hobbyists would definitely be beneficial to the breed. It is also most important that all owners, including pet owners, support their national breed clubs. Without the support of such societies, the breed would definitely experience a decline.

Although it may not be an exact replica of its original ancestors (few long-established breeds ever are), it can be categorically stated that it is a very distinctive and most impressive breed. In some ways, it is superior to its ancestral form. It enjoys a wonderful temperament and comes complete with a long and fascinating history.

The breed's appeal can't be denied when looking into the crystal blue eyes of these Russian Blue kittens.

the person reading the standard has a considerable knowledge of the breed. This is only gained via the experience of seeing many good examples, as well as those that are mediocre.

The very looseness of a standard enables a breed to change, for better or worse, over any span of time. This is why you will hear the comment, 'That breed looks nothing like it did years ago.'

HOW BREEDS CHANGE

If it is noticed that some judges prefer a cat to have, for example, a more rounded head, then breeders will exhibit, and breed for, cats that exhibit such a feature. Ultimately, it becomes a case that if a cat does not meet the needs of the current trends, then that cat will not win at shows. By this

slow process, a breed can change, sometimes dramatically so. A breed may also change if its gene pool becomes so small that outcrossing to other breeds becomes essential. This, in fact, has happened on more than one occasion in the Russian Blue.

When this happens, it will have a dramatic effect on the appearance of the breed. It takes many years to return the breed to its original state. During this period, the standard may or may not be revised to accommodate the new type. This also has happened a few times in the Russian Blue.

If a standard needs revision, it is drafted on the recommendation of the breed council, not by the registry that has adopted the standard. In this way, changes are effected by specialists in the

An adventurous youngster displays the breed's trademark athleticism and agility.

breed, though the changes still must be ratified by the appropriate committee of the registry.

BREED DESCRIPTION
The following description is not that of any single association; rather, it has been compiled after reviewing the standards of five major registries. These are

LAP CAT?
The Russian has an advantage over most longhaired breeds in respect to 'lap cat' status, yet cannot be said to be the ultimate lap cat. The dense coat of the Russian means that the cat will tend to heat up rather quickly when lying on a lap, so it will not stay there quite as long as might the very thin-coated breeds that find their owners' laps to be nice warm places. This extends to the bed, where the Russian is happy on top of the bedclothes rather than under them. Of course, nothing about any cat breed is cast in stone, so there can always be exceptions to the general rule.

Britain's Governing Council of the Cat Fancy (GCCF), Europe's Federation Internationale Feline (FIFe), America's Cat Fanciers Association (CFA), The International Cat Association (TICA), also of America, and the Australian Cat Federation (ACF). Where differences between the standards of major associations are considered to be especially important, they are discussed.

The following description should meet the needs of most owners. However, those planning to become breeders and/or exhibitors should obtain the standard(s) of the registry(ies) with which their cats are registered. In general, it can be said that American standards for the breed differ from those of Britain and mainland Europe. The Australian standards are very similar to those of Britain.

HEAD
Viewed from the front, the head has the shape of a wedge. However, in mature males the cheeks are full and give a more

rounded appearance than in the female or younger male. The muzzle is short, and in European/Australian standards the whisker pads are required to be prominent. In America, the whisker pads should not be exaggerated, thus not displaying the whisker break that is created by the prominent whisker pads where they meet the muzzle as in British and Australian cats.

The length of the nose should be no longer than the distance from the eyes to the ears, and may be slightly shorter. When viewed in profile, the top of the head should be almost flat between the ears and steadily descend in a straight line to the upper edge of the eyes. There must be no stop or break, meaning a definite indentation or sharp change of angles where the forehead meets the nose. However, the forehead should not continue in a straight line to the nose tip as in the Siamese and Oriental Shorthair. A very slight change of angle is what is required, such that the line then continues to the nose tip. In kittens, the head may appear slightly rounded and the angle of change at the forehead

Frontal head study, in which the characteristic wedge shape can be seen.

may not be fully developed.

The tip of the chin should be in the same vertical plane as the tip of the nose. This should ensure that the bite is level, meaning neither a protruding (undershot) chin nor one that is receding (overshot). Receding chins were a problem years ago, but today they are much improved.

The British, European and Australian standards do not feature the neck, which should be of a good length and appear somewhat thicker than it actually is due to the dense fur. American standards require a long and slender neck, but one

Examples of differences in the ear set: (Above) The ears are at an angle to the head, typical of the American standard. (Below) The ears are set vertical to the head, in keeping with the UK, European and Australian standards.

which appears shorter due to both the fur and the high placement of the shoulder blades.

EYES

In Britain, the eyes should be almond-shaped and are required not to be small or deep-set (which should not be construed to mean too large and in any way protruding). They will display a slight slant toward the nose.

The CFA require the eyes to be round, while TICA takes a middle path of requiring them to be almost round, but just oval enough to show an Oriental slant. They also require the eyes to be rather large, while the ACF require large eyes. All standards require the eyes to be set far apart.

EYE COLOUR

On this all standards agree. Vivid green is required. Kittens will be born with blue eyes that soon change to yellow. These start to change to green at about three or more months of age. Sometimes the change is from blue to green, and there are various shades of green from very light to a blue-green. An adult with no green in the eyes is a very serious fault.

EARS

Regarding this feature, all standards are the same except in one requirement. British, European and Australian registries require the ears to be set vertical to the

is required to be svelte. This results in a somewhat slimmer cat than those of Europe, South Africa, Australia and New Zealand.

LEGS
All standards require long legs; the only difference is that American standards add that the boning should be fine. The paws must be small and oval. There should be five toes on the front feet (to include the dewclaw) and four on the rear.

TAIL
This should be of moderate length and taper from its root to its tip. The tip should be neither blunt nor pointed. American standards require a long tail, but proportionate to body size and with a moderate base thickness (CFA) or rather thick base (TICA).

The desired shape of the eye varies from standard to standard, but all standards call for green eyes. A Russian Blue is born with blue eyes that change gradually to vivid green.

head. American associations require them to be as much on the side of the head as on the top. This gives the two types a very different facial appearance that is often more obvious in some breeding lines than in others.

In respect of size, the ears should be large and display a wide basal opening. The tips are more pointed than round and the leathers are thin and translucent. They are sparsely furnished (meaning the hairs inside the ear) while the outer surface is lightly covered with short fine hairs.

BODY
Males generally are larger than females and both should be well muscled. The body is long and graceful while the bone is of medium size. In America, fine boning is called for while the body

The Russian Blue's tail should taper from base to tip, and be of a length proportionate to the body.

COAT

This is the most important characteristic of the Russian Blue. More than any other feature, it sets it apart from all other breeds. The double coat comprises a very dense undercoat that is amply covered by a topcoat of guard and awn hairs.

Most cats have this double coat. The density in the Russian Blue is such that it should, in a good example, stand at an angle of about 45 degrees. This gives it a very plush appearance. When touched, the texture of the coat is very soft, this texture being created by the short and fine silk-like guard hairs. There should be no suggestion of coarseness.

Coat of Nebelung: The standard of TICA in America requires that the coat be of medium to long length on the body, with a fluffy tail. I am advised that, in a future revision of the standard, it may state that the texture of the coat can be silky, or coarser, with weatherproofing oils.

One of the problems that Nebelung breeders may find difficulty in achieving is the high density of the Russian Blue coat. This is because the genetic base of the longhair was of Turkish Angora type.

Coat density will require periodic crossing to the Russian Blue to attain and maintain, as is the case with the Exotic Shorthair. This will necessitate numerous Nebelung variants being produced (shorthaired individuals) or, if Nebelung to Nebelung becomes the normal, the acceptance that the breed's coat may never be as dense as in the parent breed.

TEMPERAMENT

Although not allocated points, the temperament of the breed is, uniquely among cat associations, referred to in note form in the standard of the GCCF. It states that an even-tempered cat is required. It is hoped that judges will distinguish between a temporarily upset or frightened cat that is of sound temperament, as compared to one that is clearly aggressive in its nature and therefore most undesirable.

ON THE MOVE...

The Russian Blue is neither cobby nor svelte. The consequence of this is that it is much more athletic than the Persian, Ragdoll and similar breeds, but it may not have quite the same straight-line speed as a Siamese or breeds of similar svelte stature. The Russian can jump from one shelf to the next with the best of them, and is equally adept at climbing in the vertical plane, at times to the dismay of its owners when it peers down at them from the top of the drapes. Its anatomy also enables it to maintain its periods of activity far longer than can heavier built cats—it uses less energy in its movements.

Temperament is a vital trait in the Russian Blue. A typical specimen should be active, even-tempered and tolerant.

It should be added that all cat associations, within their exhibition rules, do make similar comments regarding temperament as a general requirement for all breeds. The inclusion of this trait in the Russian Blue is merely to remind all concerned with the breed that temperament is a vital trait in this breed and must always be treated as such.

The standard of the Asian Group of the GCCF makes exactly the same comment, while in the Abyssinian, Bengal and Burmese breeds, aggressive behaviour is a specific breed fault (as it is in the Russian Blue). In the Burmese,

temperament actually is allocated points. It can be been argued that the very inclusion of such reference has only been added because it is felt that the breed has a problem and that this should be addressed. This would be incorrect—or normally so.

Any breed can have individuals of questionable temperament because of their environmental upbringing, or due to inherently poor temperament in a breeder's line. All breeders and exhibitors, and most certainly all breed judges, should be aware of this fact. This said, I feel that perhaps the wrong message is sent out to potential

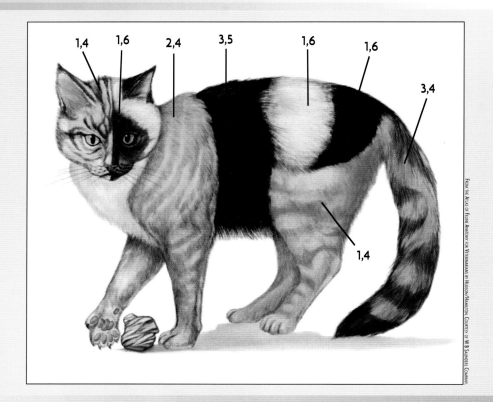

1,4   1,6   2,4   3,5   1,6   1,6   3,4   1,4

FROM THE ATLAS OF FELINE ANATOMY FOR VETERINARIANS BY HUDSON/HAMILTON. COURTESY OF W B SAUNDERS COMPANY.

PARTICOLOURED CAT

Not a new breed of feline, this 'particoloured cat' illustrates the many possibilities of the feline coat. Since cats come in three basic hair lengths, short, long and rex (curly), all three coat lengths are illustrated here. Additionally, different coat patterns, such as mackerel tabby, Abyssinian and self-coloured, are depicted to demonstrate the differences.

1–3 COAT TYPES
1 Shorthair coat
2 Rex (curly) coat
3 Longhair coat

4–6 COAT COLOUR PATTERNS
4 Mackerel (tabby)
5 Abyssinian
6 Self-coloured

breed owners when temperament is cited specifically in the standards of just a few breeds, and excluded from all others. Logic would suggest that it should only be included if there were a real need to do so.

BREED FAULTS

In the cat fancy, there are two fault types. There are those that apply to all breeds and those that are breed-specific. All-breed faults are essentially those related to anatomical problems and undesirable anomalies. Here we are concerned only with breed-specific faults, which are as follows.

A coat that is flat, thus not standing at the required angle and therefore lacking density. The CFA also adds long coat to their listing of faults. An Oriental- or Siamese-type body, or one that has the cobbiness of the British Shorthair type is desirable. A weak chin and/or an uneven bite is stated in the GCCF standard but is included in other standards indirectly because it would rank as a general all-breed fault.

With respect to colour, a major fault would be incorrect eye colour in an adult. White anywhere in blue or black varieties, together with any colour other than white in the white variety are faults. In American registries, any colour other than blue is not acceptable in this breed, or in the Nebelung, at this time.

COAT COLOUR

In most registries around the world, only the blue colour is accepted under the name of Russian. However, in the GCCF and the ACF, both white and black are also recognised.

Russian Blue: The desired shade of blue has changed over the years and presently it is required to be of a medium colour in Britain, Europe, Australia and many other countries. In America and Canada, preference is for a lighter shade. The original Russian Blue of Britain during the 19th century was probably of the shade presently required by the GCCF in Britain. The lighter shade was regarded as of a more mixed domestic ancestry based on comments made by Harrison Weir in 1892.

The colour should be clear and sound to the roots. The GCCF standard requires that there be no banding or silver tipping, though an absence of pigment at the hair tip is acceptable. This is what gives the breed its silvery sheen. The American standards require guard hairs to be distinctly tipped in silver.

Other than the choice of words, the end result is genetically the same: a lustrous silvery sheen. The nose leather should be blue to match the coat, but the paw pads may be slightly lighter in their colour. An even lighter shade is acceptable in kittens.

The blue colour is universally accepted in the breed and certainly seen the most frequently. The white and black varieties are not accepted by many registries.

The colour blue in cats is created by a double-recessive situation. Firstly, a mutation creates all black pigment while a second mutation alters the way pigment is scattered in the hair shaft. It results in some areas' having no pigment, while in other areas there is a clumping (high density) of black.

The effect of light's being scattered in the hair cells creates the illusion of the black's being diluted. The genetic symbol for blue is d, which stands for density (not dilution as is commonly assumed). The non-blue cat is represented genetically by the letter D, meaning normal density (non-dilution). A Russian Blue has the genotype aabb.

Russian White: This colour was accepted into the GCCF standard during the 1980s and presently has preliminary status, a stage that breeds and colours must pass through before attaining championship status. It must be a pure white, sound to the roots and free of any yellowing. A dark mark is acceptable on kittens and should disappear with maturity. Nose leather and paw pads should be pink.

The colour is created by a dominant gene, designated W, that, like albinism, prevents the formation of pigment. However, unlike albinism, which results in a red-eyed animal, the dominant white does not affect eye colour. This can thus display normal eye colour. A Russian White has the genotype of WW or Ww.

Russian Black: This colour was accepted at the same time as the white. It is required to be jet black to the roots. A slight rusty tinge is acceptable only in kittens. Nose leather and paw pads should be black.

Black is created by a recessive gene mutation that replaces all yellow pigment in the wild type ticked pattern (agouti) with black. The tabby is a variety of the agouti. Black is genetically repre-sented by the lowercase a, meaning non-agouti. This is the alternative gene to A, the agouti. The Russian Black has the genotype of aa.

SKIN AND HAIRCOAT OF CATS

Schematic illustration
of histologic layers of
the integument skin.

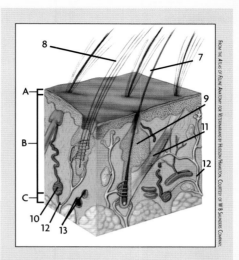

A Epidermis
B Dermis
C Subcutis

7 Primary hair
8 Secondary hairs
9 Area of sebaceous gland
10 Apocrine sweat gland
11 M arrector pili
12 Nerve fibre
13 Cutaneous vessels
14 Tactile hair
15 Fibrous capsule
16 Venous sinus
17 Sensory nerve fibres
18 External root sheath
19 Hair papilla

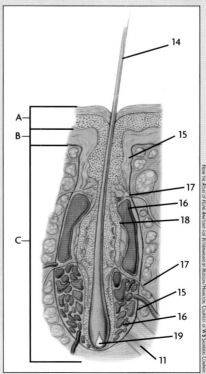

Schematic illustration of
a tactile hair (whisker).

From the Atlas of Feline Anatomy for Veterinarians by Hudson/Hamilton. Courtesy of W B Saunders Company.

From the Atlas of Feline Anatomy for Veterinarians by Hudson/Hamilton. Courtesy of W B Saunders Company.

Buying a kitten is much more than a novelty. Be sure that you understand the responsibility that comes with adding a kitten to your home.

Purchasing a
RUSSIAN BLUE CAT

Given its distinctive looks, it is no wonder that the Russian Blue has gained such a devoted following. Before the decision to purchase is made, however, careful consideration should be given to the implications and responsibilities of cat ownership. If more owners would do this, there would be far fewer half-starved pets roaming our streets or having to live in local animal rescue centres.

OWNER RESPONSIBILITY

The initial cost of a Russian Blue represents only a fraction of its lifetime's cost. The first question is, 'Can you afford one?' The kitten needs vaccinations to protect it against various diseases. Boosters are then required every year. Cat food is more costly than that for dogs. There is also the cost of cat litter every week. Periodic vet checks and treatment for illness or accidents must be allowed for. When holidays are taken, you may need to board the pet at a cattery.

From the outset, there will be additional costs apart from that of the kitten. It will need a basket, a carrying box, feeding and grooming utensils, a scratching post, a few toys and maybe a collar. If you have any doubts at all about being able to supply all these needs, it is best not to obtain a cat.

Other matters also need careful thought. If you are planning to have a family, will your love for the Russian Blue be compromised once a baby arrives? Cats generally are not a problem with family newcomers, providing they are not ignored or treated as being a threat to the baby. Never purchase a kitten for a child unless you want one yourself. If you are elderly, it is only fair to consider what would happen to your cherished pet if it were to

The most difficult and enjoyable part of your selection may be choosing between those adorable faces!

outlive you or if you were to become hospitalised for long periods.

It is most unfortunate that many people rush into the purchase of cats on impulse. They then find they cannot cope if problems, and extra costs, ensue. Some lose interest in the pet once it matures past its kitten stage. The evidence of these realities is easily seen in the growing number of cats abandoned or taken to animal shelters every year. Invariably their owners will make feeble excuses for why the cat cannot be kept. But the bottom line is that they did not stop to consider at the outset what responsible ownership entailed.

The Russian Blue is a breed that will enjoy lots of activity, so it will display an excellent learning curve. Not everything it learns will necessarily please its

THE PURCHASING PROCESS

Never rush into the purchase of a companion that is to be given the freedom of your home and will become an integral part of your life. A pure-bred cat may live 20 or more years. This is a long time. It is very prudent to take all those steps that will minimise the chances of your ever regretting the choice you make. Once you have decided on the sex, age and reason for purchase (pet, show or breeding), proceed cautiously, heeding all the advice given here. By following a planned process of selection, you will also gain much useful information.

owners, such as opening cupboard doors, climbing onto things and generally making a nuisance of itself. But we can attribute this to

One look at these soft puffs of blue with their beguiling eyes, and you will have to resist taking the whole litter home!

mischief, and what true cat lover would want to be without this aspect in a feline companion?

The genes for a more outgoing temperament, a legacy of the Siamese influence, are within the Russian Blue's genetic make-up, and may show themselves in some individuals due to the random combination of genes. However, the more likely combination produces a temperament that is toward the quieter and more shy end of the spectrum. This more reserved aspect will show in the Russian Blue's tendency to take a while to accept people and, when it does, to then go to the opposite extremes with them.

While it will get on with other cats and young children with no problems—this is a very tolerant breed—it will prefer these to be of a nature comparable to its own. Its voice is relatively quiet compared to most other breeds. It is often no more than a chirp, or even simply an opening of its mouth without an audible sound being emitted. The Russian Blue is definitely a very refined breed and has, throughout its history, always been supported more by feline connoisseurs rather than by the mainstream of pet owners.

KITTEN OR ADULT?

Most potential owners normally want a kitten because it is so cute, cuddly and playful. A kitten is

DOCUMENTATION

When you take delivery of your kitten, certain paperwork should come with it:

1. Three- to five-generation pedigree.
2. Breeder-signed registration application form or change of owner registration form. This assumes the breeder has registered stock. If they have not, the kitten cannot be registered at a later date. It is worth less than the kitten with registration paperwork. You are not recommended to purchase a kitten from unregistered parents.
3. Certificates of health, vaccination and neutering, if this has been effected. Ideally, it is desirable that the kitten's parents have been tested negative for major diseases. Additionally, the breeder should know the blood group of your kitten. This may be of importance at a later date.
4. Details of worming or other treatments attended.
5. Diet sheet, feeding timetable and brand names of food items used. This diet should be maintained for at least ten days while the kitten adjusts to the trauma of moving home.
6. Signed receipt for monies paid.
7. Signed copy of any guarantees. Not all breeders give a guarantee on the reasonable grounds that once the kitten leaves their care, its onward well-being is no longer under their control.

easily trained and has not yet developed bad habits, which the older Russian Blue may have done. This said, if you plan to breed or exhibit, there are advantages in obtaining a young adult. Other potential owners, such as the elderly, may benefit by avoiding the demanding needs of a young kitten. In both of these instances, a good age is when the youngster is 9–15 months old. Even a fully mature Russian Blue may prove an excellent choice for some owners.

Kittens should not be obtained under 12 weeks old, though 14–16 weeks is better. No reputable breeder will sell them younger than this. Less caring breeders will

A ventilated shoulder bag made for small pets is an easy-to-carry and convenient way for your Russian Blue to accompany you, whether on a trip or your daily errands.

TAKING KITTY HOME
Arrange collection of the kitten as early in the day as possible. If a long journey is involved, be sure to take a few breaks so kitty does not suffer from travel sickness. Do not make stops to show the kitten to friends; this represents a health hazard. Once home, offer the kitten a drink, then allow it to sleep if it so requires. Children must be educated to handle a kitten gently, never to tease it and to respect its sleeping privacy. Until it is litter-trained, it should be restricted to the kitchen or another room with an easy-to-clean floor surface.

let them go to new homes as young as eight weeks of age. Such juveniles will barely have been weaned. They will not have developed the needed resistance to major diseases. They are more likely to become stressed by the premature removal from their mother and siblings. Their vaccinations will not be fully effective. These factors will dramatically increase the risk of immediate problems.

GENDER SELECTION
If it is to be purely a pet, the Russian Blue's gender is unimportant. Both are delightful. Males are usually larger, bolder and more outgoing. Females tend to be more discerning about which humans

they like. However, each Russian Blue is an individual. Its character and health, more than its sex, should be the basis of selection. Again, the sex is unimportant for the potential exhibitor. It is not even necessary for the cat to be sexually 'entire.' Classes for neuters are featured in shows.

Those with breeding aspirations are advised to obtain only females. All pet owners should regard neutering (males) and spaying (females) as obligatory. Today this can be effected at any age after eight weeks.

LOOK BEFORE YOU LEAP

It is important for you to meet as many Russian Blue breeders and kittens as you can. This gives you a good mental picture of what an healthy typical example should look like and cost for the quality that you want. Normally, you will get what you pay for. If you look for the cheapest kitten, there will be a sound reason why it is the cheapest!

The best place to start your search is a cat show. Purchase the show catalogue. It lists all the exhibitors and their addresses. You can see if any live in your immediate locality. Whenever possible, it is best to purchase locally so you can visit the home of the breeder. Some breeders will insist that you do so in order to be satisfied that you will make a good owner.

AN HEALTHY KITTEN

Closely inspect any kitten before making a final decision. Keep in mind the following points:

Eyes and nose: Clean and clear with no signs of discharge.

Ears: Fresh-smelling and erect.

Coat: Healthy, not dull or dry.

Anal region: Clean with no staining of the fur.

Feet: Four toes on each foot, plus a dewclaw on the inside of each front leg.

Teeth: Correct bite.

There should be no signs of parasites or bald areas of fur. A potbelly may indicate worms.

Shows and breeders are advertised in the various cat magazines available from newsagents. You can also contact a major cat registry, which will supply a list of national and regional clubs, which are usually able to supply breeder lists. When visiting a breeder, always make an appointment. Try to visit no more than one a day. This reduces the risk that you may transport pathogens (disease-causing organisms) from one establishment to the next. Selecting a good breeder is a case of noting the environment in which the cats are kept, the attitude of the owner to you and their cats and how friendly and healthy the kittens look. It is vital that the chosen kitty has an outgoing personality. It must not appear timid or very shy. This indicates a lack of breeder socialisation or a genetic weakness in its temperament. Either way, it is not a kitten you should select.

CHOOSING A KITTEN

If you choose the breeder wisely, and especially if other owners recommend him, this will greatly reduce the risk of problems related to your making a poor choice. However, a little knowledge on what to look for will not go amiss. Observe the kittens from a distance to ensure none is unduly lethargic, which is never a good sign. If any kitten displays signs of illness, this should bring to an end any further thoughts of purchase from that source. A reputable breeder would not allow a sickly kitten to remain within its litter.

It is always advisable to select a kitten that shows particular interest in you. Russian Blues are very discerning. If both of you are drawn to each other, this will greatly enhance the bonding essential for a strong relationship.

Once a particular kitten has been selected, it should be given a close physical inspection. The eyes and nose must show no signs of weeping or discharge. The ears will be erect and fresh-smelling. The coat should look healthy, never dry and dull. There must be no signs of parasites in the fur. There will be no bald areas of fur, nor bodily swellings or abrasions. Lift the tail and inspect the anal region. This must be clean with no indication of congealed faecal matter. Any staining of the fur indicates current or recent diarrhoea.

The kitten must not display a potbelly. This may indicate worms or other internal disorders. Check the teeth to be sure of a correct bite. Bear in mind that the jawbones do not develop at the same rate. Minor imperfections may correct themselves (they may also get worse), but major faults will not. Inspect the feet to see there are four toes on each, plus a dewclaw on the inside of each front leg.

With respect to the colour, there is no link between this and health (other than deafness in certain white varieties). Any faults in the colour or its placement will only be of importance in breeding or exhibition individuals. The potential breeder/exhibitor should obtain a copy of the official standard so they are *au fait* with all colour, coat and bodily faults of the breed.

KITTY SHOPPING SPREE

Certain accessories should be regarded as obligatory and obtained before the kitten arrives at your home.

SCRATCHING POST

This will save the furniture from being abused! There are many models, some being simple posts, while others are combined with play stations and sleeping quarters. These are the best for keeping your cat interested.

LITTER BOX(ES)

Some are open trays; others are domed to provide extra privacy. Still others have special bases in which odour removers are fitted.

CAT LITTER

There are numerous types on the market, each offering advantages

CAT LITTER

The litter that is used in cat boxes can be very variable, and in many cases cats reject the use of a cat box because of the litter. Certainly, if your cat rejects the use of the cat box, you should try different litters. You can start with the litters available at your local pet shop, then you can try sand, dirt, cedar shavings or whatever will appeal to your cat. Several cat owners grow clover in a tray and their cats seem to prefer that. However, the tray is kept outdoors and the cats may simply be marking the clover tray rather than using it for elimination purposes.

and drawbacks. Avoid the low-cost types that contain a lot of dangerous dust. Use those that are fully biodegradable.

FOOD/WATER DISHES

Polished metal has the longest wear life. Earthenware is less costly than metal and superior to the plastic types.

Cat carriers are a necessity of cat ownership, though no cat welcomes the opportunity of being carted about in a crate. Nonetheless, the carrier is the only safe option for transport to the veterinary surgeon.

Double-bowl feeders are very convenient for feeding your cat. Go to your pet shop to purchase top-quality feeders, which should come in a variety of colours, styles and sizes.

There is nothing glamorous about purchasing a litter box, yet cat owners have few options in this regard. Consult your local pet shop to see a selection of boxes. Some cats do not accept a covered box, while others welcome the 'privacy.'

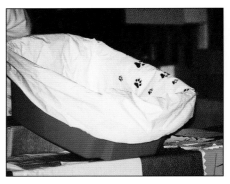

Liners are available for most litter trays to assist in keeping them clean and more manageable.

Purchasing a scratching post is a smart option for the cat owner. It's best to purchase a sturdy, well-made post that will last your cat years of utility.

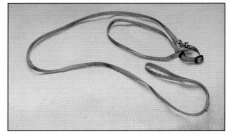

If you are considering walking your Russian Blue, you must have a lead that is suitable for a cat.

Scratching posts are made to withstand your cat's 'abuse,' so the post you select should be sturdy and covered in a safe, long-lasting material.

Your local pet shop will carry a variety of litter boxes and trays from which you can select the one best suited to your needs.

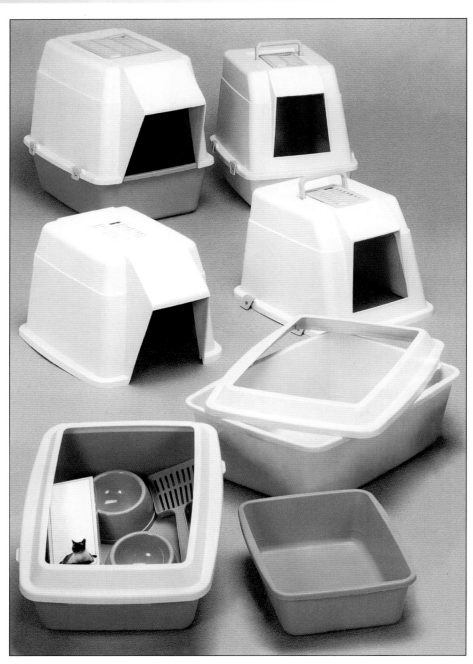

HOMEMADE TOYS

Cats love to play and pet shops have many cat toys to choose from. Sometimes, however, people give their cats homemade toys. These can be harmful to your cat, as they could have pieces that could break off and be swallowed. Only give your pet toys from the pet shop that have been proven safe for cats.

With such a variety of cat toys available, it can be as entertaining for you to watch your Russian Blue with its toys as it is for it to play with them!

You should be able to find suitable nail clippers made for cats wherever you buy grooming supplies.

GROOMING TOOLS

Among the basics are a good-quality bristle brush, a fine-toothed comb, nail trimmers and a soft chamois leather.

CAT COLLAR AND/OR HARNESS

Select elasticised collars. Be sure a name and address disc or barrel is fitted to this. A harness must be a snug but comfortable fit if it is to be effective.

CARRYING BOX

This is essential for transporting the cat to the vet or other places, as well as for home restriction when needed. Be sure it is large enough to accommodate a fully-grown Russian Blue, not just a kitten. The choice is between collapsible models, soft plastic types and, the best choice, those made of wood or fibreglass.

Purchase toys that are fun for both of you...many types of cat toys provide for interaction between the cat and a human playmate.

A kitten's curiosity and climbing ability can get it into some precarious places. Ensure your Russian Blue's safety by 'cat-proofing' your home and supervising its explorations.

RUSSIAN BLUE CAT

For a kitten, its human environment holds many dangers. Its owner must protect it from these until it becomes agile and wiser. The following dangers lurk in typical households. Always check whether there are additional potential hazards in your home. The most important decision you need to make from the outset is whether or not the kitten is to be given outdoor liberty.

HOW MUCH FREEDOM?

More than at any time in the past, the question of how much freedom a cat should be given is the subject of heated debate. It is a very subjective matter. Here the more pertinent points are given so you can relate these to your home location. This, to a very large degree, should influence your decision.

Cats living in or close to an urban area are at the highest safety risk. The amount of traffic is such that death from road-traffic accidents is a major concern. In such environments, there are high dog populations, some of which are feral. Injury or death from dog attacks is therefore another major source of danger to a feline.

Urban cat populations are also extremely high. Far too many cats are living a virtually feral existence. These are tough, streetwise cats that often carry fleas and other parasites that are vectors of disease. Some will be carriers of, or infected with, feline leukaemia and other deadly diseases.

The typical feline family pet can be badly injured if it becomes engaged in fights with these roaming bullies. Furthermore, their very presence in and around a gentle cat's garden can cause the pet severe stress. This can make it fearful of stepping outside its home. In some instances, it may cause the pet actually to leave its home.

Kittens are inquisitive and will play with almost anything they find! Make sure that your kitten doesn't discover any 'playthings' that could cause it harm.

Sadly, if these risks are not enough, there is no shortage of people who will steal a pure-bred cat, the more so if it is friendly. Add to this the number of abusive people who do not like cats roaming into their gardens, and the scenario is not good. Finally, free-roaming cats also take an heavy toll on local bird and wildlife populations.

Taking these various facts into account, the urban cat is best kept indoors. It can enjoy the benefit of the outdoors if supplied with a roomy aviary-type exercise pen. Some cats can be trained to walk on a lead. This allows outdoor enjoyment, even if this is restricted to the garden. When walking your cat in public places, use only an harness. This is much safer than a collar.

In contrast to urban situations, the cat living in a rural environment is far safer, the more so if there are no immediate neighbours or busy roads. Even so it is wise to restrict the cat's outdoor freedom to daylight hours. During the night it is more likely to get run over or to threaten local wildlife.

Those living between the extremes of isolated areas and busy urban environments should consider the local risk factor. Generally it is best to keep the cat indoors but to provide an outdoor exercise pen.

HOUSEHOLD DANGERS

Within its home, a kitten is best viewed as an accident waiting to happen! The most dangerous room is the kitchen. Hot electric hobs, naked flames from gas rings, boiling pans of food or water and sinks full of water are obvious hazards. An iron left on its board with cable trailing to the floor is an invitation to a kitten to jump up—with potentially fatal consequences. Washing machines or spin dryers with warm clothes in them, and their doors open, are inviting places to nap. Always check that the kitty isn't inside if the door has been left open. Cupboards containing poisonous or other dangerous substances should always be kept securely closed.

In the living room, the normal dangers are aquariums without hoods, unguarded fires, electric bar heaters, poisonous indoor plants, trailing electrical leads and ornaments that may be knocked over by a mischievous kitty. Toilets can be fatal to an over-curious kitten. The same is true of a bath containing water. Balconies should be safeguarded to remove the potential for the kitten to slip and fall.

OTHER DANGERS

Other potential dangers are when electric tools are left lying about and connected to power outlets—even worse if they are left on, as with bench saws. If the kitten is given freedom to exercise in a garden containing a pond, the kitten must be under constant supervision. Cherished ornaments should be placed out of reach of the kitten, as much for their safety as to any danger they may present to the kitty. It's not always the direct danger of something that can be the problem. If an ornament or similar item crashes to the floor, this can startle the kitten into a panicked departure! The kitten could then fall from a shelf in its haste. Of course, all safety measures apply equally to adult cats.

BOARDING YOUR CAT

Cats do not like to travel and the best alternative is to have a trusted friend, relative or pet-sitter watch your cat in your home. If this is impossible, then you may have to board your cat. You can get recommendations from friends or your veterinary surgeon as to which catteries are reputable. When choosing a boarding house, you should visit the facility beforehand to make certain that it is clean and quiet, and that the personnel are caring and attentive to boarders. You should also enquire about their policies concerning health, vaccinations and neutering.

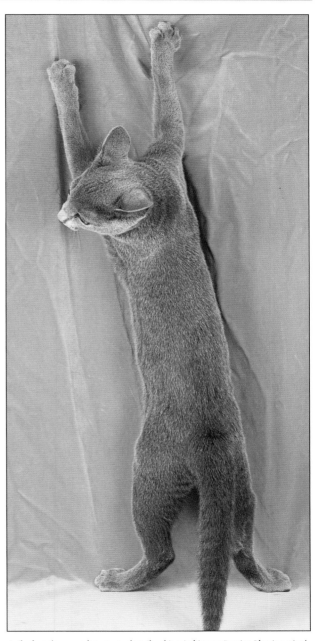

Agile doesn't seem adequate to describe this mischievous Russian Blue in action!

There is no better food for young kittens than their mother's milk.

RUSSIAN BLUE CAT

Today the feeding of cats has been reduced to its most simple level with the availability of many scientifically prepared commercial diets. However, this fact can result in owners' becoming casual in their approach to the subject. While the main object of a given diet is to provide the ingredients that promote healthy growth and maximum immunity to disease, it also fulfils an important secondary role.

A proper diet must maintain in the cat a psychological feeling of well-being that avoids nutritionally related stress problems or syndromes. By ensuring the diet is balanced, of good variety and never monotonous, these dual roles will be achieved. This approach will also avoid the situation of the cat's becoming a finicky eater.

BALANCE AND VARIETY
A balanced diet means one that contains all of the major ingredients—protein, fats, carbohydrates, vitamins and minerals—in the ratios needed to ensure maximum growth and health.

Variety means supplying foods in a range of forms that will maintain and stimulate the cat's interest in its meals. Commercially formulated foods come in three levels of moisture: low (dried), semi-moist and moist (tinned).

Generally, the dried and moist forms are the most popular. Dried cat foods have the advantage that they can be left in the cat dish for longer periods of time than tinned foods. They are ideal for supplying on a free-choice basis. Like the tinned varieties, they come in a wide range of popular flavours.

In order to meet the specific needs of a kitten, there are specially formulated foods available. These contain the higher protein levels needed by a

Feed your kitten with a diet recommended by the breeder or your veterinary surgeon.

growing kitten. As it grows, the kitten can be slowly weaned onto the adult types. There are also special brands available from vets for any kitten or cat that may have a dietary problem as well as special diets for the older cat. These may need lower ratios of certain ingredients,

IMPORTANT DON'TS

- Do not let your cat become a fussy eater. Cats are not born fussy but are made that way by their owners. Your cat will not starve if given the correct food, but it may try to convince you otherwise. However, a cat that refuses all foods offered may be ill. Contact your vet.
- Do not give a cat sweet and sticky foods. These provide no benefit and, if eaten, will negatively affect normal appetite for wholesome foods.
- Do not feed vitamin and mineral supplements to either kittens or adults unless under advice from a veterinary surgeon. Excess vitamins and minerals can be as bad for your cat's health as a lack of them. They will create potentially dangerous cellular metabolic imbalances.
- Do not give any questionable foods, such as those that smell or look 'off.' If in doubt, discard them. Always store foods in cool, darkened cupboards. Be sure all foods from the freezer and refrigerator are fully thawed.

MILK AND CATS
Milk, although associated with cats, is not needed once kittenhood has passed. Indeed, excess can create skeletal and other problems. Some cats may become quite ill if given too much. They are unable to digest its lactose content. However, small amounts may be appreciated as a treat. Goat's milk, diluted condensed milk and low-lactose milks are better than cow's milk.

such as proteins and sodium, so as to reduce the workload of the liver.

Flavours should be rotated so interest in meals is maintained. This also encourages familiarity with different tastes. Naturally, Russian Blues will display a greater liking for certain flavours and brands than for others.

FRESH FOODS
To add greater variety and interest, there are many fresh foods that Russian Blues enjoy. Some will be very helpful in cleaning the teeth and exercising the jaw muscles. All have the benefit of providing different textures and smells that help stimulate the palate. Feed these foods two or three times a week as treats or occasionally as complete meals.

Cooked poultry, including the skin but minus the bones, is

usually a favourite, as is quality raw or cooked mincemeat. Cooked beef on the bone gives the cat something to enjoy. Cooked white fish, as well as tinned tuna and sardines, are examples of ocean delights. Never feed raw fish; this can prove dangerous, even fatal. Although cats rarely enjoy items such as rice, pasta or cooked vegetables, these can nonetheless be finely chopped and mixed with meats or fish. Some Russian Blues may develop a taste for them. Various cheeses and scrambled or boiled eggs will often be appreciated—but never give raw eggs.

If the diet is balanced and varied, the addition of vitamin and mineral supplements is unnecessary and can actually prove dangerous. While certain of these compounds are released

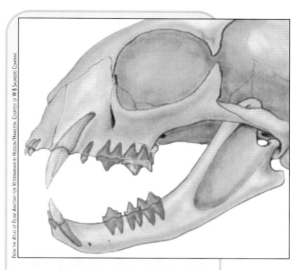

FROM THE ATLAS OF FELINE ANATOMY FOR VETERINARIANS BY HUDSON/HAMILTON, COURTESY OF W B SAUNDERS COMPANY

MEET THE MEAT-EATERS

Since cats are carnivorous, their teeth are designed to bite and cut. Except for crunching dried foods, cats do very little chewing. They have the fewest teeth of any common domestic mammal—typically 30 (although there are some variations). The canines usually are more developed than the incisors.

DIETARY DIFFERENCES BETWEEN CATS AND DOGS

You should never feed your cat dog food because dogs and cats have different dietary needs. Cats have a much higher need for fats than dogs, and kittens need more than adult cats. Cats also require unusually high levels of dietary protein as compared with those required by dogs. The foods you choose for your cat must supply these essential components.

from the body if in excess, others are not. They are stored and can adversely affect efficient metabolism. If a cat shows loss of condition and disinterest in its food, discuss its diet with a vet.

HOW MUCH TO FEED

Food intake is influenced by many factors. These are the cat's age, activity level, the ambient temperature (more is eaten in the colder months), the cat's breeding state (rearing kittens) and the quality of the food. Always follow the breeder's recommendations on diet until your kitten has settled into your home. Thereafter the needed quantity will increase as the

kitten gets older, until full maturity at about two to three years of age.

As a basic guide, a four-month-old kitten will require four meals a day. At six months old, one meal can be dropped. By twelve months of age, only two meals will be required, possibly only one if dried foods are also available on a free-choice basis. As the number of meals is decreased, the quantity must be increased at the others.

FOOD AND WATER CONTAINERS

Russian Blues are not too fussy over which vessels are used for supplying their food and water, but a few tips are useful. Russian Blues do not like to eat from dirty dishes anymore than you would. Their food bowls should be washed after each meal. Water containers should be washed every day and replenished often. Saucers make ideal food plates. Wide feeders from your pet shop are excellent for dried biscuits. Pot or polished metal containers are better buys than plastic. They last longer and are easier to keep clean.

Having a short muzzle, the Russian Blue does not like to place its head into deep food dishes nor do they like their whiskers to touch the inner walls. Ensure dishes are wide and shallow.

ESTABLISHING DAILY INTAKE

Quoting amounts needed is impossible because of a varying factors. The best way to establish requirements is on an actual consumption basis. Place a small amount of food on the dish and see how quickly this is eaten. If all is devoured within a few minutes, add a little more. Repeat this until the kitten/cat is satiated and walks away from its dish. Do likewise at the other meals and you will quickly establish daily intake.

WHERE AND WHEN TO FEED

Usually, the best place to feed a cat is in the kitchen. It is important to place food and water dishes as far away from the litter tray as possible. Feeding near the litter tray could deter the cat from eating. Cats also like to eat in quiet comfort. Meals should be spread across the entire day. When the number is reduced to two, these should be given in the morning and evening at convenient times. For the Russian Blue given outdoor freedom, it is best to feed the main meal in the evening. This encourages it to come home at this time. It can then be kept indoors overnight.

DRIED FOOD— MORE WATER

If the cat is only given dried foods, it is essential that its water bowl is always full; it will need to drink more. But it is best to give both dried and moist food types. This minimises the risk of urological problems created by pH alkalinity associated with dried diets.

Follow the breeder's advice about which brand to feed your kitten when you take it home.

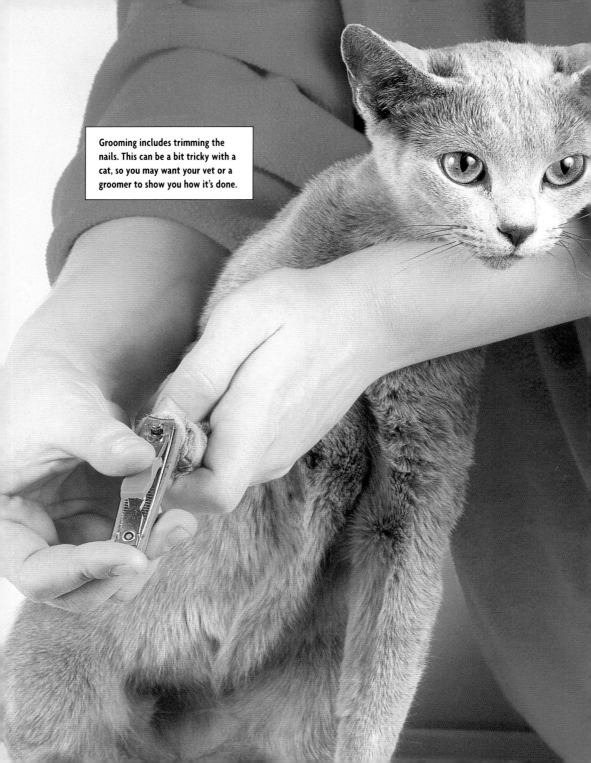

Grooming includes trimming the nails. This can be a bit tricky with a cat, so you may want your vet or a groomer to show you how it's done.

RUSSIAN BLUE CAT

The Russian Blue is unique in the cat world for its double coat, which creates its plush, very soft texture. If brushed every day, it will rarely need combing, though this is beneficial. Brisk brushing followed by a polish, using a chamois leather or piece of silk cloth, will maintain the fur in super condition.

Regular grooming also enables close examination of the cat for any signs of problems. These include fleas or mites, small wounds, abrasions, swellings and bald areas. The grooming process should include inspection of the cat's ears, teeth and nails.

BRUSHING
Place the cat on a table of an height enabling you to comfort-ably control and groom the kitty. It can be useful to place white paper on the table. If any fleas are present, you will more easily notice them if they are groomed out of the fur. If the grooming is carried out gently, cats enjoy the experience. You should start when your Russian Blue is still a kitten. Commence by brushing the fur on the back of the neck. Work along the back and down the sides, then down the legs and finally the tail.

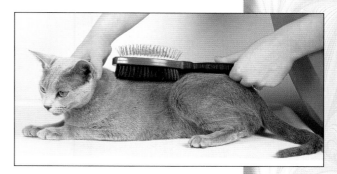

The abdominal area must be brushed more gently as it is very sensitive.

Next, repeat the process using the fine-toothed comb. First, comb against the lie of the hair. This will enable you to see if there are any parasites present. These often favour the tail base or the neck behind the ears. Next, comb with the lie of the fur. Add a final lustre by brushing with the chamois.

BATHING
Occasionally, even shorthaired cats may need bathing. This may be of the wet or dry type. For wet baths, using the kitchen sink is preferable to a bath. This saves bending and allows for better control of the cat. To prevent the cat from sliding, use a rubber mat. A spray attachment is more

The Russian Blue's splendid coat deserves to be maintained in top condition.

GROOMING EQUIPMENT

Following are the basics for an home grooming routine:

1. Semi-stiff bristle brush or rubber-pinned brush
2. Fine-toothed comb
3. Flea comb
4. Thin chamois leather and/or a silken cloth
5. Pair of guillotine-type nail trimmers
6. Medium-soft toothbrush
7. Cat toothpaste
8. Supply of cotton wool and cotton buds
9. Bottle of baby oil

available from pet shops. Alternatives would be talcum powder, powdered chalk or heated bran flakes.

The kitten should be bathed by the time it is six months of age. This will familiarise it with the process before it matures and the process degenerates into a pitched battle. Cats have no love of bathing but can come to accept it if it does not become an unpleasant ordeal.

Grooming should always precede bathing, as this will remove any dead hairs. The key to success lies in ensuring that no water or shampoo is allowed to enter and irritate the eyes or ears. You should be able to cope single-handed with a kitten. However, it may be prudent to have someone else present just in case the adult proves more of a super cat than a kitten!

The water temperature should be warm, never cold or too hot.

efficient than a jug to wet and rinse the coat. The cat should have its own towels.

The choice of shampoo is important. It should ideally be formulated for cats—do not use one for dogs. This could cause problems on a cat's coat. Baby shampoos are the best alternative. Dry shampoos in powder form are

DRY SHAMPOO

A dry bath may be preferred to a wet one during very cold weather or when the cat is not well enough for a water bath. Sprinkle dry shampoo onto the coat and give it a good brushing. This will remove excess grease and dirt without being as thorough as a wet bath. Be very sure that all of the powder is brushed from the fur to avoid potential irritation and consequential scratching.

Prepare a shampoo and water solution before commencing. Have a large towel at hand. Commence by soaking the fur of the neck, then work along the back, sides, legs and tail. Pour shampoo onto the back and work this in all directions until the cat has been fully shampooed. Next, thoroughly rinse all the shampoo away. It is essential that none be left, otherwise it may cause later irritation. Gently but firmly squeeze all water from the coat. The face can be cleaned using a dampened flannel.

Wrap the kitten in the towel and give it a brisk rubbing until it is as dry as possible. It can then be allowed to dry naturally, after which it can be given a final brush and polish. If the cat is normally allowed outdoors, do not allow this for some hours until you are sure the coat is dry. In the colder months, it is best to attend to bathing in the early evening and keep the cat indoors overnight. The use of an hand dryer is not essential on a short-coated breed, but does shorten the drying time.

EARS, EYES AND NAILS

When inspecting the ears, look for any signs of dirt. This can be gently wiped away using a dampened cotton bud or one with just a little baby or vegetable oil on it. Never attempt to probe into the ear. If the ear is very waxed, this may indicate any of various health problems. A visit to the vet is recommended. The corner of the eyes can be gently wiped with damp cotton wool to remove any dust that occasionally accumulates.

Inspection of a cat's claws is achieved by firstly restraining it while on its back on your lap or held against your chest. Hold the paw and apply pressure to the top of this with your thumb. The nail will appear from its sheath. If the nail needs trimming, use the appropriate trimmers.

It is vital that you do not cut into, or even too close to, the quick, which is a blood vessel. This can be seen as a darker area of the nail in pink-clawed cats. It is more difficult, or not possible, to see the quick in dark-coloured nails. In such instances, trim less. You may need an helper to do the trimming or the holding. If in doubt, let your vet do this for you. If cats have ample access to

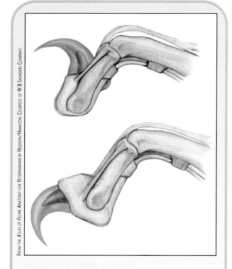

FROM THE ATLAS OF FELINE ANATOMY FOR VETERINARIANS BY HUDSON/HAMILTON. COURTESY OF W B SAUNDERS COMPANY.

RETRACTABLE CLAWS

When at rest, a cat's claws are retracted. The muscles hold the claws in their sheaths. The claw is then extended if the cat wishes to attack prey, defend itself, grab an object or climb. That is why your cat's claws are not always visible. This is true for all species of felines except the cheetah, which is unable to retract its claws, except when it is very young.

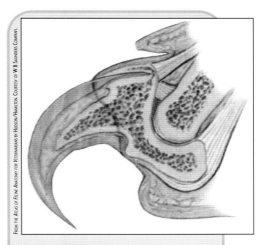

From the *Atlas of Feline Anatomy for Veterinarians* by Hudson/Hamilton. Courtesy of W B Saunders Company.

DECLAWING

Declawing is the surgical removal of all of the claw (or nail) and the first toe joint. This practice is heavily frowned upon and even illegal in some countries, such as the United Kingdom. Unfortunately, in some areas of the world this procedure is still performed. Some owners only have the claws from the front feet removed; others do all four feet.

An alternative surgical procedure is one that removes the tendon that allows the cat to protract its claws. This procedure, referred to as a tendonectomy, as compared to an onychectomy (removal of the claws), is less traumatic for the cat. Claws still must be filed and trimmed after a tendonectomy.

Declawing is not always 100% successful. In two-thirds of the cases, the cats recovered in 72 hours. Only 4–5% of the cats hadn't recovered within a fortnight. About 3% of the cats had their claws grow back!

Clean the outer ear gently, never probing into the ear canal.

Tear stains or dirt in the eye area can be removed easily with a soft wipe and a special cleansing solution available from most pet shops.

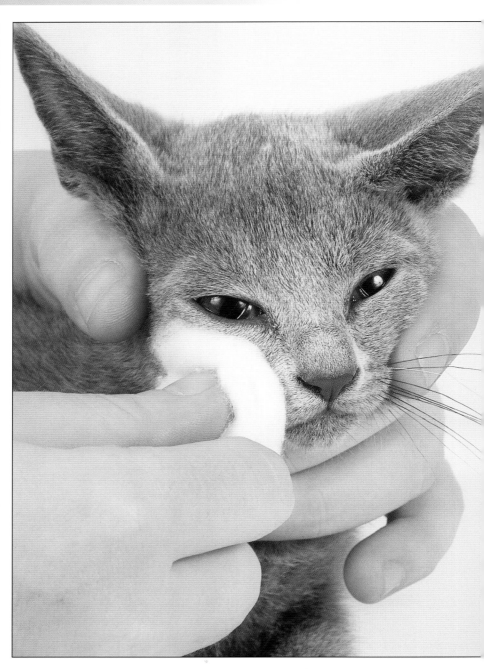

PRESS-ON NAILS!

A stylish and fairly successful inhibitor of scratching is a plastic covering on the nails. A plastic sheath is placed over each nail and glued on with a strong, permanent adhesive. Depending upon the cat's activity, these sheaths can last from one to three months.

scratching posts, they will only infrequently, if ever, require their nails to be trimmed.

TEETH

From its youngest days, your kitten should become familiar with having its teeth cleaned. Many owners do not give the teeth the attention they should. This has become progressively more important due to the soft-diet regimens of modern cats. Initially, gently rub the kitten's teeth using a soft cloth on which toothpaste has been placed. This will accustom the kitten to having its teeth touched as well as to the taste of the tooth cleaner. When this is no problem for the kitten, you can progress to a soft toothbrush and ultimately one of medium hardness. Periodically let your vet check the cat's mouth.

GINGIVITIS (Plasmocytic-Lymphocytic Stomatitis)

There are many causes of this condition. But the end result is the same—bad breath, excessive plaque, tooth loss and, almost certainly, pain. The cat salivates excessively, starts to eat less and consequently loses weight. On inspection, the gums are swollen, especially in the areas of the premolar and molar teeth. They bleed easily. There are various treatments, such as antibiotics, immunostimulants and disinfectant mouth gels. However, these invariably prove short-term and merely delay the inevitable treatment of extraction.

Prevention avoids this painful condition. Regular tooth inspection and cleaning, plus provision of hard-food items, such as cat biscuits, achieve this to a large extent. There are also special cat chews made of dried fish that help clean the teeth. They also contain antibacterial enzymes that minimise or prevent secondary bacteria from accumulating. Ask for these at your pet shop or vet's surgery. Gingivitis may commence in kittens, so do not think it is something that only occurs in older cats.

Bringing home a Russian Blue kitten means the start of a very special friendship with a very special breed of cat.

One of the outstanding virtues of cats is that they are easy to live with. They are fastidious in their personal habits related to grooming and toilet routines and basically require very little of their owners. Nonetheless, behavioural problems in cats can occur, and an owner needs to understand all of the possible causes and solutions. You may never encounter a single problem with your cat, but it pays to be prepared should your feline charge disrupt your domestic bliss.

THE BASIS OF TRAINING

The most effective means of training a cat is via reinforcement of success. A cat learning from lavish praise of doing what is required will want to repeat the action to gain more affection. There are no potential negative side effects. Conversely, when scolding or another method of discipline is used, there is always the possibility that the cat will not relate the punishment to what the owner had intended.

For example, you cannot discipline for something done in the past. The past is anything

much longer than a few minutes ago. If you call the cat to you and punish it for something done hours earlier, it cannot relate to that action. It will relate the discipline to the act of going to you when called! This will create insecurity in the pet, increasing the risk that more problems will develop.

REMEDIAL METHODS

When faced with a problem, firstly try to pinpoint the likely cause(s). Next, consider the remedial options. Be sure that these methods will not result in negative side effects linked to you. Always be the paragon of patience. Some problems may be

The cat's ultimate behaviour lies in your hands. Training should start as soon as the kitten arrives at your home.

extremely complex and deeply
rooted within the cat's behaviour
patterns. As such, they are habits
not easily changed, and often
difficult to analyse. In discussing
the following problems, it is
hoped that you will understand
the basic ways to correct these
and other unwanted patterns of
behaviour that might occur. But
always remember, it is far better
to avoid a problem than to
correct it.

CATS AND OTHER PETS

If you already have a pet cat or dog, or
almost any other animal that isn't
small, creeping or crawling, your cat
can usually be socialised so the other
pet and the cat will tolerate each other.
In many cases, cats and dogs become
quite friendly and attached to each
other, often making frequent physical
contacts, sleeping together or even
sharing each other's food.

THE TRUTH ABOUT CATS AND DOGS

Dogs were domesticated well before cats since cats only served to protect the abode of the owner from rodents, while dogs served as guards, hunters, herders, exterminators and as loyal companions that were readily trainable. Cats have always been more independent and less trainable. Cats are unique in having the scrotum fully haired, a marked difference from their canine counterparts. This led one early observer to say that cats were not small dogs!

THE LITTER TRAY

A very common problem for some owners is that their cat starts to attend to its toiletry needs anywhere other than in its litter tray. The problem may become apparent from the time the kitten gets to its new home, or it may develop at any time during its life. So, let us start from the beginning and try and avoid the situation.

Until you are satisfied that the kitten is using its litter tray, do not give it access to carpeted rooms. The youngster should already have been litter trained well before you obtained it. You should buy a litter tray similar to the one it is already familiar with. It is also important that the same brand of litter is used, at least initially. Place the tray in a quiet spot so the kitten has privacy when attending to its needs.

A kitten will need to relieve itself shortly after it has eaten, exercised or been sleeping. Watch it carefully at these times. If it stoops to attend to its needs other than in the litter tray, calmly lift it into its tray and scratch at the litter. Never shout or panic the kitty by making a sudden rush for it. If it does what is hoped, give it lots of praise. If it steps out of the tray, gently place it back in for a few seconds.

If nothing happens, be patient and wait, then repeat the process. If it fouls the kitchen floor when you are not watching, simply clean this up and wait for the next opportunity to transport the kitten to its tray. It rarely takes long for a kitten to consistently use this. Be very sure the tray is kept spotless. Cats have no more desire to use a fouled toilet than you do. Every few days, give the cat tray a good wash, using soapy water and always rinsing it thoroughly. Allow it to dry, then fill the tray with litter to a depth of about 4–5 cms (1.5–2 inches).

By identifying the cause(s) of litter-box problems, the correction is often self-evident. However, once the cause has been corrected, this is only part of the solution. Next, the habit of fouling other places must be overcome. When possible, do not let the cat enter rooms it has started to foul until the odour

TEN CAUSES OF LITTER-BOX PROBLEMS

1. The litter tray is dirty. Cats never like to use a previously fouled tray.
2. The litter has been changed to one of a different texture that the cat does not like. Generally the finer-grained litters are the most favoured.
3. A scented litter is being used to mask odours. The cat may not like the scent. Such litters should not be necessary if the tray is regularly cleaned.
4. The tray is regularly cleaned, but an ammonium or pine-based disinfectant is being used. This may aggravate the cat's sensitive nasal mucous membranes. Additionally, the phenols in pine are dangerous to cats.
5. The litter tray is located too close to the cat's food and water bowls. Cats do not like to eat near litter trays or to defecate/urinate close to their feeding areas.
6. Another cat or free-roaming pet has been added to the household and is causing the cat stress. In multi-cat households, two or more trays may be needed.
7. There is insufficient litter in the tray. There should be about 5 cms (2 ins) of litter depth.
8. The cat has developed a fear of using the tray due to an upsetting experience. For instance, the owner may have caught the cat as it finished using the tray in order that it could be given a medicine. Children may be disturbing it while it is relieving itself.
9. The cat is ill (or elderly) and is unable to control its bowel movements. Veterinary attention is required.
10. The cat, because of one or more of the previous problems, has established other more favourable areas.

has had time to fully disperse. Wash the area of the fouling, then treat carpets and soft furnishings with an odour neutraliser (not an air freshener) from your pet shop or vet.

If the cat cannot be prevented from entering certain rooms, then cover previously fouled areas with plastic sheeting or tinfoil, or rinse the fouled area with white vinegar (which cats hate!). Also, place a litter tray in the fouled room while the retraining is underway. It may help if a different size, type or colour of tray is used.

SCENT MARKING

Both sexes scent mark, though males are more prolific. It is a means of advertising their presence in a territory, thus an integral part of their natural behaviour. Spraying is usually done against a vertical surface. It tells other males that the individual is residing in that territory. Alternatively, it will tell a female that a male lives close by—or it will tell the male that a female is in the area. It is thus a very important part of a cat's social language.

Neutered cats have little need

Litter-box training is the key to clean living with your cat.

to mark their territory, or leave their 'calling card' to attract mates. They are far less likely to spray than those not altered.

However, scent marking may commence when the cat is attempting to assert its position in the household.

CAUSES OF SCENT MARKING

1. Another cat, or pet, has been introduced to the household. It may be bullying the resident cat. This problem may resolve itself when the two get to know each other. The more cats there are, the longer it may take for the situation to be resolved. Much will depend on the space within which the cats may roam and whether they are able to avoid those they dislike.
2. The birth of a new family member may annoy the cat for a while, especially if its owner suddenly gives it less attention.
3. A friend staying in the home for a few days may not like cats. If 'shooed' away a number of times, the cat may feel it should assert its position and mark it.
4. If the cat is given outdoor freedom, a bully may have moved into the pet's territory. Having lost control of its own garden, the pet may assert its territorial boundaries within its home. If a cat flap is used, another cat may be entering the home and this will trigger the resident to scent mark.

MARKING TERRITORY

Cats are geographical by nature and they mark their territories in the usual way...by spraying their urine. The frequency of spraying is amazing! A non-breeding male cat that is not within its own turf will spray about 13 times an hour while travelling through the new territory. A breeding male will spray almost twice as much. One report states that free-ranging males spray 62.6 times an hour—that's more than once a minute!

Cat urine is recognisable for at least 24 hours and male cats spend a lot of time sniffing the area. Females spend less time, but both sexes easily recognise the urine from male cats that are strange to the area.

To overcome the problem of scent marking, you first need to try and identify if there is an obvious specific cause. In multi-cat households, it also requires positive identification of the sprayer(s) and the favoured spraying surface. Giving the cat more freedom may help, and its own sleeping place if it does not have one. Covering the sprayed surface with plastic sheeting, or a cloth impregnated with a scent the cat does not like (such as lemon, pepper or bleach), may be successful. Spraying the cat with a water pistol when catching it in the action is a common ploy.

Veterinary treatment with the hormone progesterone may prove effective—discuss this with your vet.

SCRATCHING

Scratching is a normal feline characteristic. Unfortunately, house cats tend to destroy the furniture to satisfy their need to scratch. Feral or outdoor cats usually attack a tree because trees are readily accessible and the bark of the tree suits their needs perfectly. If the outdoor cat lives in a pride, it will scratch more than a solitary feral cat. The reasons for this are known. When

TIDY TOILETING

During the kitten's stay in the nest box, the mother will assist or even stimulate bowel and urine elimination, at least for the first month of the kitten's life. The mother also does the clean-up work in the nest box. But once the kitten is older, it becomes capable of relieving itself out of the nest box. Usually the kitten likes sand, soft earth or something that seems absorbent and is easily moved with its paws. By the time the kitten is two months old, it should develop the discipline of covering its elimination. Not all kittens develop this discipline, though the use of an absorbent clay litter seems to be helpful in developing this discipline in young cats. Your local pet shop will have various cat litters to offer you.

THE PICA SYNDROME

The term 'pica' is a veterinary term that refers to a morbid desire to ingest things that are abnormal to the cat's diet. Cats are often addicted to soft materials like wool, silk, cotton or a mixture of these and synthetic cloths. Hard plastics, wood and even metals have been involved in this pica syndrome. If you observe your cat chewing these fabrics or materials, speak to your vet. Most vets who observe the pica syndrome think it is a nervous problem that can successfully be treated with drugs normally used for depression. In any case, the genetic makeup of your cat should be investigated and if pica occurs in any of the parents or previous offspring, do not breed your cat.

Some more elaborate scratching posts are combined with toys or perches, as shown here, to keep the cat's mind and claws occupied.

cats scratch, they leave telltale marks. Parts of the nail sheaths exudate from glands located between their claws, and the visual aspects are the marks, which cats leave to impress or to advertise their presence.

Cat owners whose cats scratch

SETTING THE GROUND RULES

From the outset, you must determine the ground rules and stick to them. Always remember that your companion's patterns of behaviour begin to form from the moment it first arrives at your home. If the adult cat is not to be given outdoor freedom in the future, then do not let it outdoors as a kitten. If any rooms are to be out of bounds to the adult, then do not let the kitten into them. Stability is vital in a cat's life; without it, the result will be stress and its related behavioural changes.

Ground rules of how to handle the kitten and to respect its privacy when sleeping should be instilled into all children. The cat's meals should be given at about the same time each day. This will have the secondary advantage that the pet's toilet habits will be more predictable.

should not consider the scratching as an aggressive behavioural disorder. It is normal for cats to scratch. Keeping your cat's claws clipped or filed so they are as short as possible without causing bleeding may inhibit scratching. Your vet can teach you how to do this. Clipping and filing should be started when the kitten is very young. Starting this when the cat has matured is much more difficult and may even be dangerous.

There are ways to control annoying cat scratching. Certainly, the easiest way is to present your cat with an acceptable cat scratching post. These are usually available at most local pet shops. The post should be covered with a material that is to your cat's liking. If your cat

With some training and patience on your part, your Russian Blue kitten will behave as 'picture perfect' as he looks!

has already indicated what it likes to scratch, it usually is a good idea to cover the post with this same material. Veterinary surgeons often suggest that you use sandpaper, as this will reduce the cat's nails quickly and it will not have the urge to scratch. Certainly using hemp, carpeting, cotton towelling or bark is worth a try. Once the cat uses the post, it usually will have neither a desire nor a need to scratch anyplace else.

Besides the physical need to scratch, many cats have a psychological need to scratch. This is evidenced by where they scratch versus what they scratch. Often cats prefer semi-darkness. Some prefer flat surfaces and not vertical surfaces. Some prefer public areas in which their human friends are present instead of secluded areas. It may be stress-related, as with scent marking, because scratching is another territory-marking behaviour. In any case, the idea is to get your cat to scratch the post and not the carpets, furniture, drapes or the duvet on your bed.

Introduce your cat to the post by rubbing its paws on the post, hoping it will take the hint. Oftentimes the cat voluntarily attacks the post. Unfortunately, oftentimes it doesn't. If you catch your cat scratching in a forbidden area, startle it with a loud shout, banging a folded newspaper

FERAL CATS

Feral cats are, as a general rule, undernourished. They spend most of their time searching for food. Consequently, those feral cats that have kittens spend less time with their kittens than do well-nourished cats. It has been shown that kittens born to feral mothers are usually unsocial and show little affection for their mothers. Obviously, they would show a similar lack of affection for a human. That's one of the reasons that feral kittens make poor pets and should neither be adopted nor taken into your home. Kittens that for any reason are separated from their mothers at the age of two weeks develop an attitude of fear and wariness. They escape from contact with other cats or humans and can even be dangerous if they feel trapped.

against your hand, or something which will take its attention away from scratching. Never hit the cat. This will only get a revengeful reaction that might be dangerous.

RUBBISH RUMMAGING

Cats are inquisitive and may decide to have a good look through any interesting rubbish bins that are exuding enticing odours. Normally, the answer is to remove the bin. However, if the attraction always seems to be to the kitchen rubbish, there may be a nutritional problem. The cat may be searching for food because it is being underfed! It may alternatively be receiving an unbalanced diet and is trying to satisfy its inner need for a given missing ingredient.

Another possibility, and one which may be more appropriate to the indoors-only cat, is boredom or loneliness. These conditions can only be remedied by greater interaction between owner and cat and/or obtaining a companion feline.

Clearly, the cause should be identified. The immediate solution is to place the rubbish in a cupboard or similar place that is out of the cat's reach. This type of solution is called removal of the re-enforcer. It is a common method of overcoming problems across a number of unwanted behaviours. However, it does not correct the underlying problem, which must still be addressed.

The first-time cat owner should not think that the problems discussed will likely be encountered. They are only met when the cat's environment is lacking in some way. Always remember that the older cat may have problems with bowel control. An extra litter tray at another location in the home will usually remedy this situation. Finally, if a problem is found and you are not able to remedy it, do seek the advice of your vet or breeder.

The goal of breeding always should be to pass on the best traits of a breed, and improve the breed if possible, from generation to generation.

Breeding Your

RUSSIAN BLUE CAT

While the idea of becoming a breeder may appeal to many owners, the reality is more difficult than is often appreciated. It requires dedication, considerable investment of time and money and the ability to cope with many heart-wrenching decisions and failures.

It would be quite impossible to discuss the complexities of practical breeding in only one chapter, so we will consider the important requirements of being a breeder plus basic feline reproductive information. This will enable you to better determine if, indeed, this aspect of the hobby is for you.

BEING A BREEDER

Apart from great affection for the breed, a successful breeding programme requires quantifiable objectives. Foremost among these is the rearing of healthy kittens free from known diseases. Next is the desire to produce offspring that are as good as, indeed better than, their parents.

Such objectives ensure that a breeder will endeavour to maintain standards and reduce or remove from the breed population

any instances of dangerous diseases and conditions. Only stock registered and tested free of major diseases should ever be used. Adopting such a policy helps to counteract those who breed from inferior and often unhealthy cats.

To be a successful breeder, you will need to become involved in the show-competition side of the hobby. Only via this route will you be able to determine if your programme is successful or not. Always remember that even the top-winning breeders still produce quite an high percentage of kittens that will only be of pet-quality. There will be many disappointments along the road to even modest success.

THE DISADVANTAGES OF BREEDING

There are many rewards to be gained from breeding, but the

A litter of Russian Blue kittens has undeniable appeal, but that alone is not enough reason to attempt breeding.

disadvantages also should be carefully considered. Kittens are demanding, especially once they are over three weeks of age. Rearing, vaccination, registration and veterinary bills will be costly. Any thoughts of profit should be dispelled. Homes must be found for the kittens, which will entail receiving many telephone calls— some at very inconvenient hours.

Many potential buyers will prove to be either unsuitable or 'time wasters' looking for the cheapest pedigreed cat obtainable. Kittens may die, while cats of any age could test positive for a major disease. They may have to be put to sleep or given to a caring person who understands the problem.

Owning a number of cats will mean investing in cat pens. When females come into heat, they will try to escape and mate with any local tom with a twinkle in his eye! Their scent and calls will attract roving Romeos who will gather near your home and

TOM FOOLERY

A non-neutered male cat kept as a single pet has little or no value for breeding purposes. It must be exhibited so it can gain some fame. The owner must have modern facilities to house both males and females. Females are always serviced at the home of the stud owner. This is extra responsibility and cost.

Such a male cannot be given any freedom to roam. If the tom is kept indoors, its scent-marking odours will often become intolerable. Even kept outdoors in a suitable cat pen, it will spray regularly to attract the attention of any females in the area. Toms are more assertive and often more aggressive than neutered males. If they are allowed any outdoor freedom, they will become involved in battles with the local toms. Consequently, they will soon lose their handsome looks!

Most cat breeders do not even keep males because of the problems and costs they entail. These cats are best kept in catteries where the owners have the time, the funds and everything else needed to justify their retention.

Consider the care of one kitten... and then consider how that multiplies with each kitten in a litter!

involve themselves in a series of raucous battles. Holidays and matings will need to be planned around hoped-for litter dates. All in all, owning only one or two breeding females is a major commitment.

Before deciding whether

breeding really is something you want to do, what would make good sense would be to neuter the pet and then become an exhibitor. When you have exhibited a number of times, your knowledge of cats will be greater, as will your contacts. You will be more aware of what quality is all about and what it will cost for a well-bred female. It will be like an appren-

If you decide to breed a litter, you must be committed to finding good homes for the kittens. As a breeder, you must ensure that new owners have the best interests of the breed in mind, just as you do.

ticeship. Whether you then become a breeder, remain an exhibitor or prefer life as a pet owner, you will be glad you heeded the words of advice given here.

STOCK SELECTION

Stock selection revolves around health, quality, sex and age. Before these are discussed, it should be stated that many beginners unwisely rush this process. It is essential that ample time be devoted to researching from whom to purchase. This decision will influence a novice breeder's entire future endeavours.

TOO MANY CATS

There are already too many cats in the world. In many countries, thousands of pathetic-looking felines can be seen wandering the streets in a badly emaciated state. They live tormented lives and have become a major social problem in many areas. There can be no excuse for these feral populations in developed Western nations. Quite frankly, some people who own cats, including some pedigreed owners, lack a sense of responsibility.

Cats allowed to roam in a non-neutered state are by far the main reason for the overpopulation problem. Unless a cat is of show or breeding quality, there is not a single justification for it to be bred or to remain in a non-neutered state. If your cat was purchased as a pet, you should help to resolve this global problem by having it neutered at the earliest possible date. This will make it a far healthier, happier and less problematic pet.

CAT CALLS

Females left in a non-spayed state are far more at risk from diseases and infections of the uterus. When in heat, the female becomes unusually affectionate and provocative. Her calls, a sound once heard never forgotten, can become extremely annoying if she is left unmated.

THE MALE STUD

The selection of a suitable stud should have been planned months before, as it can take some time to find the best male to use. It is preferred that the breeding lines of the stud are compatible with those of the female, meaning that both pedigrees will carry a number of the same individuals in them. This is termed line-breeding. The ideal male will excel in those features that are considered weak in the female. You may read in other books that if a female is weak in a given feature, the ideal stud will be the total opposite. However, this can be misleading.

If the female has an overly long tail, what you do not need is a stud with a short tail. Rather, his tail should be as near the ideal length as possible. Genetically, this will improve tail length in your line without introducing unwanted genetic variance in your stock. Compensatory matings, such as short tail to long tail, will create such a variance. Once a male has been selected, ensure that all his papers and vaccinations are in order. The female will be taken to the stud and left with him for a few days.

stock should be current on all vaccinations and worm treatments. Additionally, its blood type should be known so as to avoid incompatibility problems.

HEALTH

Cats should only be obtained from a breeder whose stock has been tested negative for the cat diseases known as FeLV, FIP and FIV. The

QUALITY

This must come in two forms. One is in the individual cat's appearance; the other is in its genetic ability to pass on the

on those looks to her offspring. Another cat that is very sound may pass on most of her good points and thus be more valuable for breeding. Of course, all litters will be influenced by the quality of the tom used. He will account for 50% of the offspring's genes. When viewing a litter of kittens,

A sound, healthy, beautiful litter is what every breeder hopes to achieve.

THE BREEDING QUEEN

A female used for breeding purposes is called a queen. The principal requirement of such a cat is that she is an excellent example of the breed. This does not mean that she must be a show winner. Many a winning exhibition cat has proved to have little breeding value. This is because a show cat gains success purely on its appearance; however, it may not pass those looks to its offspring.

A good breeding female may lack that extra something needed to be a top winner. Yet, she may pass on most of her excellent features to her offspring. Much will depend on the breeding line from which she was produced. Therefore, any potential breeder must research existing breeders to ascertain which have good track records of producing consistently high-quality cats. In truth, and sadly, few newcomers in their haste to become breeders make this extra effort. This can result in becoming disillusioned if the female produces only average to inferior kittens.

quality of its parents. The best way of obtaining these paired needs is to obtain initial stock from a breeder having a proven record of success with Russian Blues. Being well acquainted with the breed's standard will be advantageous when seeking foundation stock. A female show cat attains her titles based on her appearance, but she may not pass

CAVEAT EMPTOR

When purchasing a kitten for breeding, make certain that the seller knows what your intentions are. If a kitten is registered on the non-active register, this means it was not considered by its breeder to be good enough for breeding. Any kittens bred from such a cat cannot be registered. You should also check that the mother of the kitten/young adult in which you are interested has tested negative for FeLV, FIP and FIV and that all other vaccinations are current.

never forget that they are the result of the genes of two cats.

SEX

The beginner should obtain only females. The best advice is to commence with just one very sound female. By the time you have exhibited her and gained more knowledge about the finer points of the breed, you will be better able to judge what true

quality is all about. By then, you also will have made many contacts on the show circuit. Alternatively, you may decide breeding is not for you and will have invested the minimum of time and money.

A male is not needed until a breeder has become established. Even then, owning one is not essential to success. There is no shortage of quality studs. Males create many problems that the novice can do without. Once experience is gained is the time to decide if owning a male would be of any particular benefit.

AGE

There is no specific age at which stock should be purchased, but the following are suggested:
1. Most people purchase young kittens so they can enjoy them. However, with such youngsters, their ultimate quality is harder to assess.
2. Chances are improved if a kitten has already won awards in shows. This will be when

ROAMING ROMEOS

Males cats, toms, have extended testicles very early in life. By about nine months of age, the tom is capable of mating with a queen. Both queens and toms are polygamous and it is not uncommon for a queen to have a litter containing kittens fathered by different toms.

THE HEAT IS ON

Most female cats reach sexual maturity by the time they are 28 weeks old. Females normally accept males from late winter to early fall, about a six-month period. They have a reproductive cycle of about two weeks and are in heat for about one of the two weeks. Intercourse causes the female to ovulate and pregnancy may last for about 64 days, perhaps longer in cold climates and shorter in the tropics.

WHAT'S A PEDIGREE WORTH?

When choosing breeding stock, never be dazzled by a pedigree. No matter how illustrious this is, it is only ever as good as the cat that bears it. If the cat is mediocre, then its prestigious pedigree is worthless from a breeding perspective. There are many other pitfalls for the novice when judging the value of a breeding line. These you must research in larger, more specialised books.

she is 14 weeks to 9 months of age, but she will be more costly.
3. A quality young female that has already produced offspring is a prudent choice but will be the most expensive option.

THE BREEDING PROCESS

Sexual maturity in cats may come as early as four months of age. Breeding should not be considered until the female is at least 12 months old, especially in the slow-maturing breeds such as those of Persian and European stock ancestry. A young cat barely out of her kitten stage may not have the required physical or psychological stability to produce and raise a vigorous litter. After her first heat, a female will normally come into heat again every two to three weeks and continue to do so until mated.

The actual oestrus period lasts three to eight days. It is during this time that she is receptive to a male.

Once the mating has been successful, the time between fertilisation and birth of the young, known as the gestation period, is in the range of 59 to 67 days, 63 or 64 days being typical. The litter size will generally be two to five. Kittens are born blind and helpless, but develop rapidly. Their eyes open about the seventh day. By 21 days, they start

The quality of the kittens is based on the quality of the parents. Breeders must select their stock with utmost care and, likewise, potential owners must research the lineage of the kittens.

NEWBORN KITTENS

Most kittens are born with body hair. Their ears and eyes, however, remain closed for about two weeks, though some ears and eyes become functional after 72 hours. Kittens should be allowed to nurse for seven weeks, longer if they will not readily eat and drink from a plate. If allowed to nurse, most kittens will stay on their mother's milk for two months or more.

exploring. At this time, they will also be sampling solid foods. By eight weeks, they can be vaccinated and neutered if required. Weaning normally commences by the age of six weeks and is completed within two to three weeks.

Kittens can go to new homes when 12 weeks old, though 14 to 16 weeks is preferred. During this period, you must decide if you wish to register the kittens or merely 'declare' them. This allows them to be registered at a later time. Obtain the necessary information and forms from your cat-registration authority. You should also consider the benefits of registering your own breeder prefix. This, however, is only worthwhile if you intend to breed on a more than casual basis. If you have decided that certain kittens are unsuitable for showing/breeding, do consider early neutering.

These expressive Russian Blue babies are bursting with curiosity and ready to explore!

A sound kitten of quality breeding and an interest in showing are all you need to give exhibiting a try. Showing your Russian Blue is something in which the whole family can be involved.

RUSSIAN BLUE CAT

Without shows, the cat fancy could not exist. There would be only an handful of breeds as compared with today's ever-growing list. There would be fewer colour patterns and far less awareness about cats. Given the great importance of shows to the cat fancy, it is perhaps a little surprising, and also disappointing, that the majority of cat owners have never visited a feline exhibition.

Shows such as the National and the Supreme of Britain, or their equivalents in other countries, are the shop windows of the world of domestic cats. They are meeting places where breeders from all over the country compete to establish how well their breeding programmes are developing. A show is also a major social event on the cat calendar.

Whether a potential pet owner or breeder of the future, you should visit one or two shows. It is a great day out for the whole family. Apart from the wonderful selection of breeds, there are also many trade stands. If a product is available, it will be seen at the large exhibitions.

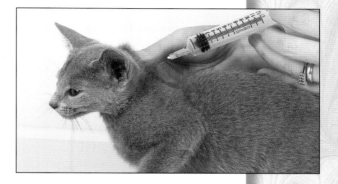

Many of the national clubs and magazines have stands. The two major shows mentioned are held in the winter months, usually November and December. However, there are hundreds of other shows staged during the year in various parts of the country. They range from small local club events to major championship breed shows and are usually advertised in the cat magazines. Your ruling cat association can also supply a list of shows.

SHOW ORGANISATION

So that you will have some idea of how things are organised, the following information will be helpful. You will learn even more by purchasing the show catalogue.

Health is as important as quality in feline exhibitions. All cats entered in a show must be vaccinated and pass an examination by a veterinary surgeon.

This contains the names and addresses of the exhibitors and details of their cats. It also lists the prizes, indicates the show regulations and carries many interesting advertisements.

A major show revolves around three broad categories of cats:

1. Unaltered cats, meaning those that are capable of breeding.
2. Neuters.
3. Non-pedigreed cats.

There is, thus, the opportunity for every type of cat, from the best of Russian Blues to the everyday 'moggie' pets, to take part. These three broad categories are divided into various sections. For example, the unaltered and neuters are divided into their respective sections, such as Longhair, Semi-Longhair, British, Foreign, Siamese and so on.

There are many more classes other than those mentioned. These include club classes and those for kittens and non-pedigreed cats.

JUDGING

There are two ways cats can be judged. One is pen judging, the other is bench or ring judging. In Britain, pen judging is the normal method, though bench judging is used for Best in Show. In pen judging, the judge moves around the cat pens. The cat gaining the most points when compared to the standard wins. In bench

judging, stewards take the cats to the judge.

If a cat wins its class, it then competes against other class winners. By this process of elimination, a cat may go on to win the Best of Breed award. It then competes against other breed winners for the Best in Group award. The group winners compete for the Best in Show award.

A breeder can gather a number of awards during the course of a show. Even those who do not own the very best cats can

ON THE CONTINENT AND BEYOND...

In Britain, the title of UK Grand Champion or Premier is won in competition with other Grand titleholders. In mainland Europe, cats can become International Champions. More British cats are expected to become International Champions with the recent introduction of passports for cats, allowing cats to compete more freely on the Continent and beyond. In countries other than Britain, the way in which shows are organised and titles achieved do differ somewhat. However, they broadly follow the outline discussed here.

take pride in gaining second, third, fourth and recommended, especially if won at the larger shows. By progression, the top cat at a show will win its class, its breed and its section, and ultimately become the Best in Show exhibit. The titles a cat can win commence with that of Champion (or Premier in the case of neuters). A Grand Champion is made after winning in competition with others of its same status. The same applies to a Grand Premier. The judging system may vary from one country to another, but the basis remains as outlined.

THE SHOW CAT

When a cat is seen preening in its pen, the hard work that has gone into its preparation is rarely appreciated. Exhibits must be in peak condition and their coats in full bloom. The potential exhibit must be trained gradually to spend hours within its show pen. It must display no fear or aggression towards strangers, such as the stewards or the judges. These must be able to physically examine it, including its ears and teeth; it also involves being lifted into the air. If a cat scratches or bites a judge, or any other show official, it is automatically withdrawn from the show. A repeat of this in the future would result, in most instances, in the cat's show

career being terminated by the ruling association.

Apart from being comfortable with people peering into its pen,

EXAMPLES OF CLASSES AT SHOWS

Open	Cats of the specified breed.
Novice	Cats that have never won a first prize.
Limit	Cats that have not won more than first prizes.
Junior	Cats over nine months of age but less than two years on the day of the show.
Senior	Cats over two years old.
Visitors	Cats living a given distance away from the show venue.
Assessment	Experimental breeds, which have approved standards.
Aristocrat	Cats with one or two Challenge Certificates so are not yet full Champions (or Premiers for neuters).

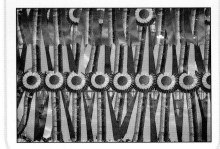

BECOMING AN EXHIBITOR

Before any hobbyist enters a show, he is advised to join a local cat club. Here, hobbyists will meet local breeders who will not only assess their cats for them but also provide help on many other topics. The novice exhibitor could attend one or two shows with an exhibitor in order to learn the ropes. During this period, he can become familiar with the show rules and regulations. These are quite extensive, intended to safeguard the best interests of the hobby, the exhibitors and, most importantly, the cats.

It is of interest to note that some breeders own cats in partnership with other fanciers. This is useful when one person enjoys the breeding side and the other the exhibition side. It enables both to be really involved in the hobby to a level that might not have been possible for either on his own. So, whether you fancy being an exhibitor or you just love cats, do make a point of visiting the next major show in your area.

the cat must be able to endure long journeys to the show venue. Unless trained, the cat may become a nervous, aggressive feline that will have a very short show career.

Obviously, the cat must display quality. This means having none of the major faults that would prevent it from gaining a first prize. These are listed in the breed standard. The meaning of quality is very subjective. You do not need to own a potential champion to be a successful exhibitor. The cat must also be registered with the association under whose rules the show is being run. In Britain, this will be the Governing Council of the Cat Fancy (GCCF) or The Cat Association of Britain.

As in anything competitive, exhibits can gain prizes at the lower levels of an hobby without

CLASSES FOR NON-PEDIGREED CATS

For non-pedigreed cats there are many classes, which include those for single colours, bicolours, tabbies, half-pedigreed, and so on. In this section, there are many delightful classes, such as those for cats owned by pensioners, by young children (by age group), best original stray or rescued cat, best personality, most unusual-looking, most photogenic and best older cat. Within this cat section can be seen some truly gorgeous felines. There is no doubt that the pet classes have been the springboard that has launched many a top breeder into the world of pedigreed cats.

having any realistic chance of winning awards in the major shows. Owning such exhibits is often part of a top breeder/exhibitor's portfolio from his early days in the hobby. Others may never move beyond the smaller shows but still gain reputations for owning sound stock. They thoroughly enjoy being involved at their given level.

If the idea of exhibiting appeals to you, the best way to make a start is to join a local club. There, you not only will be advised on all procedures but also will be able to make many new friends. Exhibiting can be costly in cash and time, but you can focus on the more local shows while attending the larger ones as a visitor.

'VETTING IN'

In England, cats are examined by a veterinary surgeon upon arrival to a show to make sure that they appear healthy. This process is called 'vetting in.' If the cat is rejected, it cannot be exhibited again until it receives a 'clearance certificate.' The possible reasons for rejection are stated in the rule book, which can be obtained at the show.

Aside from your care and regular attention from the vet, the best way to assure your cat's health is to start with an healthy kitten.

Maintaining a cat in the peak of good health revolves around the implementation of a sound husbandry strategy. At the basic level, this means being responsible about feeding, cleanliness and grooming. However, in spite of an owner's best efforts in these matters, cats may still become ill due to other causes. Although owners can attempt to prevent, identify and react to problems, only a vet is qualified to diagnose and suggest and/or effect remedies. Attempts by owners or 'informed' friends to diagnose and treat specific diseases are dangerous and potentially life-threatening to the cat.

SELECTING A VETERINARY SURGEON

Your selection of a veterinary surgeon should be based upon his reputation for skills with small animals as well as upon his convenience to your home. You want a vet who is close because you might have emergencies or need to make multiple visits for treatments. You want a vet who

has services that you might require such as nail clipping and bathing, as well as sophisticated pet supplies and a good reputation for ability and responsiveness. There is nothing more frustrating than having to wait a day or more to get a response from your veterinary surgeon.

All veterinary surgeons are licenced and their diplomas and/or certificates should be displayed in their waiting rooms. There are, however, many veterinary specialities that usually require further studies and internships. There are specialists in heart problems (veterinary cardiologists), skin problems

Your relationship with your cat's vet will begin in kittenhood and last through the cat's life. Choose a skilled vet who is close by and with whom you feel comfortable.

KEEPING YOUR CAT HEALTHY

Although there are a multitude of ailments, diseases and accidents that could befall a cat, all but the most minor of problems can be avoided with good management. The following tips are a recipe for keeping your cat in the peak of health.

- Make sure it is vaccinated and in other ways protected from each of the major diseases. It must also receive annual boosters to maintain immunity.
- Have periodic checks made by your vet to see if your cat has worms.
- Ensure that the cat receives an adequate diet that is both appealing and balanced.
- Have the kitten neutered if it is not to be used for breeding.
- Ensure that the cat's litter tray, food/water vessels and grooming tools are always maintained in spotless condition.
- Do not let your cat out overnight or when you are away from home.
- Always wash your hands after gardening or petting other people's pets.
- Groom your cat daily. If this is done, you will more readily notice fleas or other problems than if grooming was done less frequently.
- Never try to diagnose and treat problems that are clearly of an internal type. Remember, even the most informed of breeders is not a vet and unable to diagnose problems reliably for you or advise treatments. Contact your vet.
- If you are ever in doubt about the health of your cat, do not delay in discussing your concerns with your vet. Delays merely allow problems to become more established.

(veterinary dermatologists), teeth and gum problems (veterinary dentists), eye problems (veterinary ophthalmologists) and x-rays (veterinary radiologists), as well as vets who have specialities in reproduction, nutrition and behaviour. Most veterinary surgeons do routine surgery, such as neutering and stitching up wounds. When the problem affecting your cat is serious, it is not unusual or impudent to get another medical opinion, although in Britain you are obliged to advise the vets concerned about this. You might also want to compare costs among several veterinary surgeons. Sophisticated health care and veterinary services can be very costly. It is not infrequent that important decisions are based upon financial considerations.

PREVENTATIVE MEDICINE

It is much easier, less costly and more effective to practise preventative medicine than to fight bouts of illness and disease. Properly bred kittens come from parents who were selected based upon their genetic disease profile. Their mothers should have been vaccinated, free of all internal and external parasites and properly nourished. For these reasons, a visit to the veterinary surgeon who cared for the queen is recommended. The queen can pass on disease resistance to her kittens, which can last for eight to ten weeks. She can also pass on parasites and many infections. That's why it is helpful to know about the health of the queen.

VACCINATIONS

Most vaccinations are given by injection and should only be done by a veterinary surgeon. Both he and you should keep a record of the date of the injection, the identification of the vaccine and the amount given. The first vaccination is normally given when the kitten is about 8–9 weeks old. About 30 days later, a booster is given. Although there are many diseases to which a cat may fall victim, the most dangerous three—FIE, FVR and FeLV—can be safeguarded against with a single (three-in-one) injection. Thereafter, an annual booster is all that is required.

MAJOR DISEASES

There are a number of diseases for which there is either no cure or little chance of recovery. However, some can be prevented by vaccination. All breeders and owners should ensure kittens are so protected.

FELINE INFECTIOUS ENTERITIS (FIE)

This is also known as feline panleukopenia, feline distemper and feline parvovirus. The virus

NEUTERING

Neutering is a major means of avoiding ill health. It dramatically reduces the risk of males' becoming involved in territorial battles with the dangers of physical injury and disease transference. It makes the male more placid and less likely to scent mark his home. It also reduces the incidence of prostate problems, and there is no risk of testicular cancer. The female avoids potentially lethal illnesses related to her being allowed to remain in an unmated condition, such as breast cancer.

Neutering is usually performed between four and six months of age, but it can be done as early as eight weeks of age. Data available on the age at which a kitten is neutered indicate that early neutering has more advantages than drawbacks. Breeders should have this performed on all cats sold as pets.

Male cats are neutered. The operation removes the testicles and requires that the cat be anaesthetised. Females are spayed. This is major surgery during which the ovaries and uterus are removed. Both males and females should be kept quiet at home for about seven to ten days following the procedure, at which time the vet will remove the sutures.

attacks the intestinal system. It is spread via the faeces and urine. The virus may survive for many years in some environments. The use of household bleach (sodium hypochlorite) for cleaning helps to prevent colonisation. Signs, among others, are diarrhoea, vomiting, depression, anorexia and dehydration. Death may occur within days. A vaccine is available from the vet.

CARE OF FELINE KIDNEYS
The kidney of the cat is larger than that of the dog, but it has the typical bean shape. It receives 25% of the blood output of the heart! For this reason, it has rather significant veins to accommodate this large supply of blood, and injuries suffered by the kidneys are usually serious and not uncommon.

FELINE VIRAL RHINOTRACHEITIS (FVR) & CALCIVIRUS (FCV)
Also known as cat flu, this is a complex of upper respiratory diseases. Signs are excessively hard sneezing, runny nose and mouth ulcers. Cats vaccinated after having contracted flu may recover but may suffer from recurrent bouts, especially if they become stressed.

FELINE LEUKAEMIA VIRUS (FeLV)
This is an highly infectious viral disease. It is spread via direct

HEALTH AND VACCINATION TIMETABLE

Age	6 wks	8 wks	10 wks	12 wks	16 wks	6 mos	1 yr
Worm control	✔	✔	✔		✔		
Neutering						✔	
Rhinotracheitis	✔	✔		✔	✔		✔
Panleukopenia	✔	✔		✔			✔
Calcivirus		✔			✔		✔
Feline Leukaemia				✔			✔
Feline Infectious Peritonitis				✔	✔		✔
Faecal evaluation						✔	
Feline Immunodeficiency testing							✔
Feline Leukaemia testing				✔			✔
Dental evaluation		✔				✔	
Rabies				✔	✔		✔

Vaccinations are not instantly effective. It takes about two weeks for the cat's immune system to develop antibodies. Most vaccinations require annual booster shots. Your veterinary surgeon should guide you in this regard.

DISEASE REFERENCE CHART

	What is it?	Cause	Symptoms
Feline Leukaemia Virus (FeLV)	Infectious disease; kills more cats each year than any other feline infectious disease.	A virus spread through saliva, tears, urine and faeces of infected cats; bite wounds.	Early on no symptoms may occur, but eventually infected cats experience signs from depression and weight loss to respiratory distress. FeLV also suppresses immune system, making a cat susceptible to almost any severe chronic illness.
Rabies	Potentially deadly virus that infects warm-blooded mammals.	A bacterium, often carried by rodents, that enters through mucous membranes and spreads quickly throughout the body.	Aggressiveness, a blank or vacant look in the eyes, increased vocalisation and/or weak or wobbly gait.
Feline Infectious Enteritis (FIE) *aka Panleukopenia*	Highly contagious virus, potentially deadly.	Ingestion of the virus, which is usually spread through the faeces of infected cats.	Most common: severe diarrhoea. Also vomiting, fatigue, lack of appetite, severe inflammation of intestines.
Feline Viral Rhinotracheitis (FVR)	Viral disease that affects eyes and upper respiratory tract.	A virus that can affect any cat, especially those in multiple-cat settings.	Sneezing attacks, coughing, drooling thick saliva, fever, watery eyes, ulcers of mouth, nose and eyes.
Feline Immuno-deficiency Virus (FIV)	Virus that reduces white blood cells.	An infection spread commonly through cat-fight wounds.	Signs may be dormant for years or innocuous, such as diarrhoea or anaemia.
Feline Infectious Peritonitis (FIP)	A fatal viral disease, may be linked to FeLV and FIV.	Bacteria in dirty litter boxes; stress may increase susceptibility in kittens.	Extremely variable; range from abdominal swelling to chest problems, eye ailments and body lesions.
Feline Urological Syndrome (FUS)	A disease that affects the urinary tracts of cats.	Inflammation of bladder and urethra.	Constipation, constant licking of penis or vulva, blood in urine (males), swollen abdomen, crying when lifted.

CLEANLINESS IS THE KEY

Crucial to the prevention and spread of disease is the need to maintain meticulous cleanliness, especially relating to the litter tray. Many diseases and problems are transferred via faecal matter. Once a problem is suspected, the advice of a vet should be sought. Blood tests, faecal microscopy and other testing methods are now available. They can mean the difference between life and death of a cherished pet.

contact—mutual grooming, saliva, feeding bowls, faeces, urine and biting. It can be passed prenatally from a female to her offspring. It creates tumours, anaemia, immune system depression, pyrexia (high temperatures), lethargy, respiratory disease, intestinal disease and many other potentially fatal problems. It is most prevalent in high-density cat populations. Not all cats will be affected, but they may become carriers.

Kittens less than six months old are especially vulnerable. Infected cats usually die by the time they are three to four years old. Cats can be screened or tested for this disease. Vaccination is not 100% effective but is recommended in kittens being sold into multi-cat environments.

FELINE IMMUNODEFICIENCY VIRUS (FIV)

This causes the white blood cells to be significantly reduced, thus greatly suppressing the efficiency of the immune system. It is not transferable to humans. Infection is normally gained from cat-fight wounds; thus, outdoor males are at the most risk. A cat diagnosed via blood tests as FIV-positive may live a normal life for months or years if retained indoors and given careful attention. Signs may be innocuous in the early stages, such as anaemia or diarrhoea. No vaccine is available.

FELINE INFECTIOUS PERITONITIS (FIP)

This viral disease is invariably fatal once contracted in its more potent forms. However, the virulence of the virus is variable and may by destroyed by the immune system. Stress may increase susceptibility in kittens. It may be linked to FeLV and FIV. Signs are extremely variable and range from abdominal swelling to chest problems, eye ailments to body lesions. There are various

> **STRESS TEST**
>
> Stress reduces the effectiveness of the immune system. Seemingly innocuous conditions may develop into major problems or leave the cat more open to attack by disease. Stress is difficult to identify specifically, but its major causes are well known. These include incorrect diet, intrusion by another cat in its home or territory, excessive handling and petting, disturbed sleep, uncomfortable home temperatures, bullying by another cat or pet, parasitic infestation, boarding in a cattery, travel, moving, boredom, limited accommodation space and, for some felines, being exhibited.

tests available but none is as yet 100% conclusive. Strict cleanliness is essential, especially of litter trays. No vaccine is available.

FELINE UROLOGICAL SYNDROME (FUS)

This is a very distressing condition caused by an inflammation of the bladder and urethra. Signs are constipation-like squatting and attempts to urinate, regular licking of the penis or vulva, blood in urine (males), swollen abdomen, crying when lifted and urinating in unusual places (often only in small amounts).

The numerous causes include infection, dirty litter tray of the indoor cat, alkaline urine (in cats it should be acidic), diet too dry, lack of water intake (even though this may be available) and being hit by a vehicle (damaged nerves). Veterinary treatment is essential or the condition could be fatal due to the bladder's bursting or the presence of dangerous bacteria.

RABIES

Britain and most European Community countries are free of this terrible disease. The stringent quarantine laws of Britain are such that vaccination is not necessary. However, the introduction of passports for dogs and cats means that resident British cats must be vaccinated if they are to travel abroad and return to the UK without being placed into quarantine. The vaccination is given when the kitten is three or more months old. The pet passport process takes at least six months to complete, so plan well ahead.

COMMON HEALTH PROBLEMS

DERMATITIS (ECZEMA)

Dry, lifeless coat, loss of coat, tiny scabs over the head and body, loose flakes (dandruff) and excessive scratching are all commonly called eczema. The cause covers a range of possibilities including diet, parasitic mites such as *Cheyletiella spp*, fungus or an allergy to flea or other bites. Sometimes reasons are unknown. Veterinary diagnosis and treatment are required.

RINGWORM (*DERMATOPHYTOSIS*)

This problem is fungal, not that of a worm. The most common form is *Microsporum canis*, which accounts for over 90% of cases. Cats less than one year old are at the highest risk, while longhaired breeds are more prone to the problem than shorthaired cats. The fungi feed on the keratin layers of the skin, nails and hair. Direct contact and spores that remain in the environment are the main means of transmission.

Typical signs are circular-type bald areas of skin, which may be flaked and reddish. The coat generally may become dry and lifeless, giving the appearance of numerous other skin and hair

A DELICATE HEART

A cat's heart is as delicate as a human's heart, but it is much smaller. At full maturity, a queen's heart weighs between 9–12 grammes. The tom's heart is heavier, weighing 11–18 grammes. The blood that circulates through the heart chambers does not supply the heart muscle, thus requiring a separate circulatory system for the heart muscle.

POSSIBLE SOURCES OF EAR PROBLEMS
- Fight scratches
- Excess secretion of wax
- Swellings and blood blisters (haematoma) resulting from intrusion by foreign bodies (grass, seeds, etc.)
- Sunburn
- Whitish-coloured ear mites (*Otodectes cynotis*)
- Orange-coloured harvest mites *(Trombicula autumnalis)*
- Fleas
- Bacterial infection of either the outer or middle/inner ear

problems. Veterinary diagnosis and treatment, either topical or via drugs, is essential as the condition is zoonotic, meaning that it can be transferred to humans.

EAR PROBLEMS

Most of the common ear problems affect the outer ear. The telltale sign is the cat's constant scratching of the ears and/or its holding the ear to one side. Greasy hairs around the ear, dark brown wax (cerumen) in the ears, scaly flakes in or around the ear or minute white or orange pinhead-like bodies (mites) in the ear are common signs. Canker is a term used for ear infections, but it has no specific meaning.

Over-the-counter remedies for ear problems are ineffective unless

Although you should tend to your cat's ears regularly at home, the vet will also examine them thoroughly during routine check-ups.

correct diagnosis has been made. It is therefore better to let the vet diagnose and treat the cat. Some serious problems may require anaesthesia and minor surgery.

DIARRHOEA

This is a general term used to indicate a semi-liquid to liquid state of faecal matter. Mild to acute cases may be due to a change of environment, dietary change, eating an 'off' item, gorging on a favoured food, stress or a minor chill. These often rectify themselves within days. Chronic and persistent diarrhoea may be the result of specific diseases. Any indication of blood in the faecal matter must be considered dangerous.

In minor cases, withholding food for 12–24 hours, or feeding a simple diet, may arrest the condition. If not, contact your vet. Faecal analysis and blood testing may be required. By answering

A LONG, HEALTHY LIFE

As veterinary surgeons make medical advances in the health care of cats, the longevity of the typical house cat is improving. Certainly ages between 15 and 18 years are not uncommon, and reports of cats living more than 20 years are predictable.

numerous questions related to the cat's diet, general health, level of activity, loss of appetite, etc., the vet will determine whether tests are required or if immediate treatment is warranted. Do not give cats human or canine intestinal remedies; these could prove dangerous.

CONSTIPATION

When a cat strains but is unable to pass motions, this is indicative of various causes. It may have hairballs, may have eaten a bird or rodent and has a bone lodged in its intestinal tract, may be suffering from a urological problem rather than constipation or may have been hit by a car and has damaged the nerves that control bowel movements. As constipation is potentially serious, veterinary advice should be sought. Laxatives and faecal-softener tablets may be given, the faecal matter can be surgically removed or another treatment can be carried out.

THE RIB CAGE

Cats usually have 13 pairs of ribs. The ribs in the middle are longer than the ribs on either end (or beginning) of the rib cage. The first nine ribs are joined to the chest bone (sternum) with costal cartilages. Ribs 10, 11 and 12 are also associated with cartilage, which contributes to the costal arch. The thirteenth rib is called the floating rib and its cartilage is separate from the other ribs.

EXTERNAL PARASITES

FLEAS

Of all the problems to which cats are prone, none is more well known and frustrating than fleas. Indeed, flea-related problems are the principal cause of visits to veterinary surgeons. Flea infestation is relatively simple to cure but difficult to prevent. Periodic flea checks for your cat, conducted as well as annual health check-ups, are highly recommended. Consistent dosing with anthelmintic preparations is also advised. Parasites that are harboured inside the body are a bit more difficult to eradicate, but they are easier to control.

To control a flea infestation, you have to understand the flea's life cycle. Fleas are often thought of as a summertime problem but centrally heated homes have changed the life-cycle patterns, and fleas can be found at any time of the year. Fleas thrive in hot and humid environments; they soon die if the temperature drops below 2°C (35°F). The most effective method of flea control is a two-stage approach: one stage to kill the adult fleas, and the other to control the development of pre-adult fleas. Unfortunately, no single active ingredient is effective against all stages of the life cycle.

Flea prevention is a challenge to cat owners in most places. This is an adult male flea.

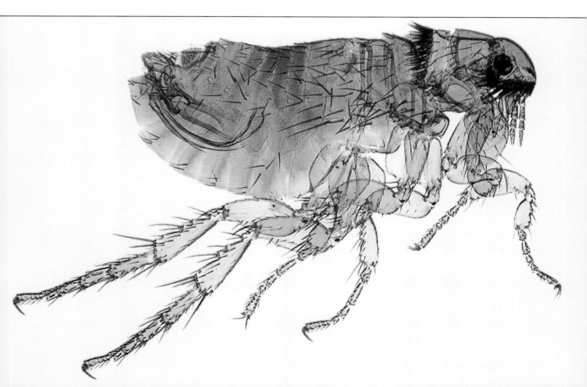

A Look at Fleas

Fleas have been around for millions of years and have adapted to changing host animals. They are able to go through a complete life cycle in less than one month, or they can extend their lives to almost two years by remaining as pupae or cocoons. They must have a blood meal every 10-14 days, and egg production begins within 2 days of their first meal. The female cat flea is very prolific and can lay 2000 eggs in her lifetime!

Fleas have been measured as being able to jump 300,000 times and can jump 150 times their body length in any direction, including straight up. Those are just a few of the reasons why they are so successful in infesting a cat!

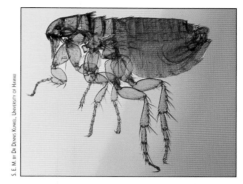

A scanning electron micrograph (S. E. M.) of a flea.

Magnified head of a flea.

LIFE CYCLE STAGES

During its life, a flea will pass through four life stages: egg, larva, pupa and adult. The adult stage is the most visible and irritating stage of the flea life cycle, and this is why the majority of flea-control products concentrate on this stage. The fact is that adult fleas account for only 1% of the total flea population, and the other 99% exist in pre-adult stages, i.e. eggs, larvae and pupae. The pre-adult stages are barely visible to the naked eye.

THE LIFE CYCLE OF THE FLEA

Eggs are laid on the cat, usually in quantities of about 20 or 30, several times a day. The female adult flea must have a blood meal before each egg-laying session. When first laid, the eggs will not cling to the cat's fur, as the eggs are not sticky. They will immediately fall to the floor or ground, especially when the cat moves around or scratches.

Once the eggs fall from the cat onto the carpet or grass, they will hatch into yellow larvae, approximately 2 mms long. This takes from 5 to 11 days. Larvae are not particularly mobile and will usually travel only a few inches from where they hatch. However, they do have a tendency to move away from light and heavy traffic—under furniture, in the carpet and behind doors are common places to find high quantities of flea larvae.

The flea larvae feed on dead organic matter, including adult flea faeces, until they are ready to change into adult fleas. Fleas will usually remain as larvae for around seven days, becoming darker in colour. After this period, the larvae will pupate a protective cocoon. While inside the pupae, the larvae will undergo metamorphosis and change into adult fleas. This can happen within a week, but the adult fleas can remain inside the pupae waiting to hatch for up to six months. The pupae are signalled to hatch by certain stimuli, such as physical pressure—the pupae's being stepped on, heat from an animal's lying on the pupae or increased

Opposite page: A scanning electron micrograph of a flea, magnified more than 100x. This image has been colorized for effect.

THE INTERNAL OPTION
Flea-killers are poisonous. You should not spray these toxic chemicals on areas of a cat's body that he licks, including his genitals and his face. Flea killers taken internally are a better answer, but check with your vet in case internal therapy is not advised for your cat.

carbon dioxide levels and vibrations—indicating that a suitable host is available.

Once hatched, the adult flea must feed within a few days. Once the adult flea finds an host, it will not leave voluntarily. It only becomes dislodged by grooming or the host animal's scratching. The adult flea will remain on the host for the duration of its life unless forcibly removed.

TREATING THE ENVIRONMENT
AND THE CAT
Treating fleas should be a two-pronged attack. First, the environment needs to be treated; this includes carpets and furniture, especially the cat's bedding and areas underneath furniture. The environment should be treated with an household spray containing an Insect Growth Regulator (IGR) and an insecticide to kill the adult fleas. There are also liquids, given orally, that contain chitin inhibitors. These

TOXIC COMBOS
Never mix flea-control products without first consulting your veterinary surgeon. Some products can become toxic when combined with others and can cause serious or fatal consequences.

PHOTO BY CAROLINA BIOLOGICAL SUPPLY/PHOTOTAKE

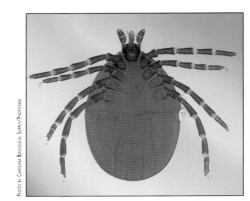

A brown tick, *Rhipicephalus sanguineus*, **is an uncommon but annoying tick found on cats.**

render flea eggs incapable of development. There are also both foam and liquid wipe-on treatments. Additionally, cats can be injected with treatments that can last up to six months. Emulsions that have the same effect can also be added to food. The advanced treatments are only available from veterinary surgeons.

The IGRs actually mimic the fleas' own hormones and stop the eggs and larvae from developing into adult fleas. There are currently no treatments available to attack the pupa stage of the life cycle, so the adult insecticide is used to kill the newly hatched adult fleas before they find an host. Most IGRs are active for many months, while adult insecticides are only active for a few days.

When treating with an household spray, it is a good idea to vacuum before applying the product. This stimulates as many pupae as possible to hatch into adult fleas. The vacuum cleaner should also be treated with a flea

The head of a tick, *Dermacentor variabilis*, **enlarged and coloured for effect.**

PHOTO BY DR. DENNIS KUNKEL, UNIVERSITY OF HAWAII

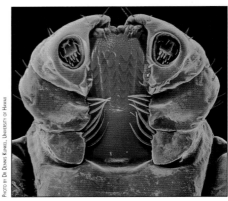

Dwight R Kuhn's magnificent action photo, showing a flea jumping.

treatment to prevent the eggs and larvae that have been hoovered into the vacuum bag from hatching.

The second stage of treatment is to apply an adult insecticide to the cat, usually in the form of a collar or a spray. Alternatively, there are drops that, when placed on the back of the cat's neck, spread throughout the fur and skin to kill adult fleas. A word of warning: Never use products sold for dogs on your cat; the result could be fatal.

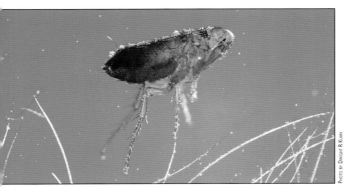

PHOTO BY DWIGHT R KUHN

The Life Cycle of the Flea

Eggs

Larvae

Pupa

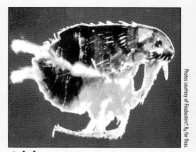

Adult

Photos courtesy of Fleabusters® Rx for fleas.

Flea Control

IGR (INSECT GROWTH REGULATOR)

Two types of products should be used when treating fleas—a product to treat the pet and a product to treat the home. Adult fleas represent 1% of the flea population. The pre-adult fleas (i. e. eggs, larvae and pupae) represent 99% of the flea population and are found in the environment; it is in the case of pre-adult fleas that products containing an Insect Growth Regulator (IGR) should be used in the home.

IGRs are a new class of compounds used to prevent the development of insects. They do not kill the insect outright, but instead use the insect's biology against it to stop it from completing its growth. Products that contain methoprene are the world's first and leading IGRs. Used to control fleas and other insects, this type of IGR will stop flea larvae from developing and protect the house for up to seven months.

EN GARDE:
CATCHING FLEAS OFF GUARD!

Consider the following ways to arm yourself against fleas:

• Add a small amount of pennyroyal or eucalyptus oil to your cat's bath. These natural remedies repel fleas.

• Supplement your cat's food with fresh garlic (minced or grated) and an hearty amount of brewer's yeast, both of which ward off fleas.

• Use a flea comb on your cat daily. Submerge fleas in a cup of bleach to kill them quickly.

• Confine the cat to only a few rooms to limit the spread of fleas in the home.

• Vacuum daily...and get all of the crevices! Dispose of the bag every few days until the problem is under control.

• Wash your cat's bedding daily. Cover cushions where your cat sleeps with towels, and wash the towels often.

Opposite page:
The tick,
Dermacentor
variabilis, **is one**
of the most
common ticks
found on cats.
Look at the
strength in its
eight legs! No
wonder it's hard
to detach them.

TICKS AND MITES

Though not as common as fleas, ticks and mites are found all over the tropical and temperate world. They don't bite like fleas; they harpoon. They dig their sharp proboscis (nose) into the cat's skin and drink the blood. Their only food and drink is your cat's blood. Cats can get potentially fatal anaemia, paralysis and many other diseases from ticks and mites. They may live where fleas are found and they like to hide in cracks or seams in walls wherever cats live. They are controlled the same way fleas are controlled.

The *Dermacentor variabilis* may well be the most common tick in many geographical areas, especially those areas where the climate is hot and humid. The other common ticks that attack small animals are *Rhipicephalus sanguineus, Ixodes* and some species of *Amblyomma.*

Most ticks have life expectancies of a week to six months, depending upon climatic conditions. They can neither jump nor fly, but they can crawl slowly and can range up to 5 metres (16 feet) to reach a sleeping or unsuspecting animal.

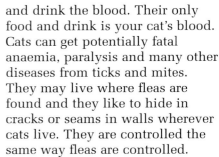

TOXOPLASMOSIS AND PREGNANT WOMEN

Toxoplasmosis is caused by a single parasite, *Toxoplasma gondii*. Cats acquire it by eating infected prey, such as rodents or birds, or raw meat. Obviously, strictly indoor cats are at less risk of infection than cats that are permitted to roam outdoors. Symptoms include diarrhoea, listlessness, pneumonia and inflammation of the eye. Sometimes there are no symptoms. The disease can be treated with antibiotics.

The only way humans can get the disease is through direct contact with the cat's faeces. People usually don't display any symptoms, although they can show mild flu-like symptoms. Once exposed, an antibody is produced and the person builds immunity to the disease.

The real danger to humans is that pregnant women can pass the parasite to the developing foetus. In this case, the chances are good that the baby will be born with a major health problem and/or serious birth defects. In order to eliminate risk, pregnant women should have someone else deal with the litter-box duties or wear gloves while taking care of the litter box and wash hands thoroughly afterwards.

INTERNAL PARASITES

Most animals—fishes, birds and mammals, including cats and humans—have worms and other parasites that live inside their bodies. According to Dr Herbert R Axelrod, the fish pathologist, there are two kinds of parasites: dumb and smart. The smart parasites live in peaceful cooperation with their hosts (symbiosis), while the dumb parasites kill their hosts. Most of the worm infections are relatively

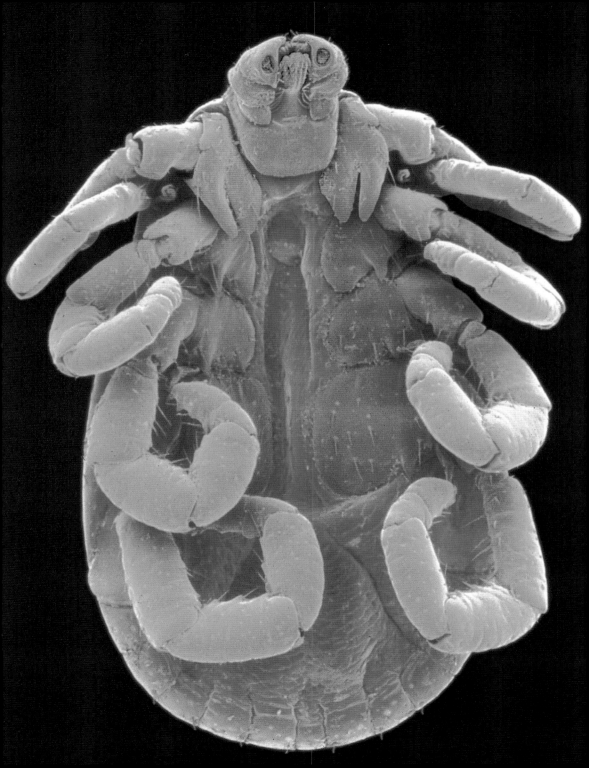

easy to control. If they are not controlled, they weaken the host cat to the point that other medical problems occur, but they are not dumb parasites.

HOOKWORMS

The worm *Ancylostoma tubaeforme* can infect a cat by larva's penetrating the cat's skin. It attaches itself to the small intestine of the cat, where it sucks blood. This loss of blood could cause iron-deficiency anaemia.

Outdoor cats that spend much of their time in the garden or in contact with soil are commonly infected with hookworm. There is another worm, the *Gordius* or horsehair worm, that, if ingested by a cat, causes vomiting.

TAPEWORMS

There are many species of tapeworms. They are carried by

DEWORMING
Ridding your kitten of worms is VERY IMPORTANT because certain worms that kittens carry, such as tapeworms and roundworms, can infect humans.

Breeders initiate a deworming programme at or about four weeks of age. The routine is repeated every two or three weeks until the kitten is three months old. The breeder from whom you obtained your kitten should provide you with the complete details of the deworming programme.

Your veterinary surgeon can prescribe and monitor the programme of deworming for you. The usual programme is treating the kitten every 15–20 days until the kitten is positively worm-free.

It is advised that you only treat your kitten with drugs that are recommended professionally.

fleas! The cat eats the flea and starts the tapeworm cycle. Humans can also be infected with tapeworms, so don't eat fleas! Fleas are so small that your cat could pass them onto your hands, your plate or your food and thus make it possible for you to ingest a flea that is carrying tapeworm eggs.

While tapeworm infection is not life-threatening in cats (smart parasite!), it can be the cause of a

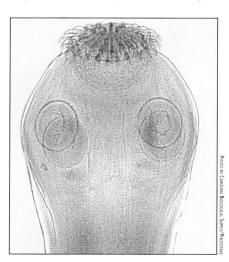

The head and rostellum (the round prominence on the scolex) of a tapeworm, which infects cats and humans.

PHOTO BY CAROLINA BIOLOGICAL SUPPLY/PHOTOTAKE

INTERNAL PARASITES OF CATS

NAME	DESCRIPTION	SYMPTOMS	ACQUISITION	TREATMENT
Roundworm (*Toxocara cati* and *Toxascaris leonina*)	Large, white, coil-like worms, 5–10 cms (2–4 inches) long, resembling small springs.	Vomiting, pot belly, respiratory problems, poor growth rate, protruding third eyelids, poor haircoat.	Ingesting infective larvae; ingesting infected mammals, birds or insects; a queen with *Toxocari cati* nursing kittens.	Anthelmintics; scrupulously clean environment (e.g. daily removal of all faeces recommended).
Physaloptera species	2–15 cms (1–6 inches) long, attacks the wall of the stomach.	Vomiting, anorexia, melena.	Eating insects that live in soil (e.g. May beetles).	Diagnosed with a gastroscope; treated with pyrantel pamoate. Prevention of exposure to the intermediate hosts.
Gordius or Horsehair worm	15-cm (6-inch) pale brown worms with stripes.	Vomiting.	May ingest a worm while drinking from or making contact with swimming pools and toilet bowls.	Anthelmintics; avoiding potentially infected environments.
Hookworm (*Ancylostoma tubaeforme*)	The adult worms, ranging from 6 to 15 mms (2.5–6 inches) in length, attach themselves to the small intestines.	Anaemia, melena, weight loss, poor haircoat.	Larva penetrating the cat's skin, usually attacks the small intestine. Found in soil and flower gardens where faecal matter is deposited.	Fortnightly treatment with anthelmintics. Good sanitation (e.g. daily cleanup of litter boxes).
Tapeworm (*Dipylidium caninum* and *Taenia taeniformis*)	Up to 91 cms (3 feet) long. Parts shaped similar to cucumber seeds. The most common intermediate hosts are fleas and biting lice.	No clinical signs—difficult to detect.	Eating infected adult fleas. Uses rodents as hosts.	Praziquantel and epsiprantel. Management of environment to ensure scrupulously clean conditions. Proper flea control.

Magnified
heartworm
larvae,
*Dirofilaria
immitis.*

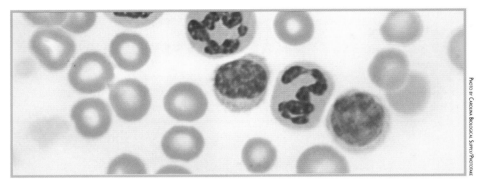

The
heartworm,
*Dirofilaria
immitis.*

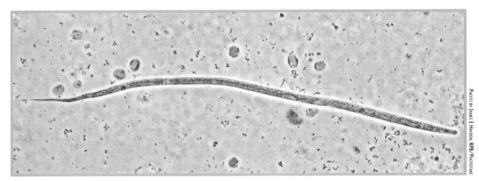

very serious liver disease for humans. About 50 percent of the humans infected with *Echinococcus multilocularis*, a type of tapeworm that causes alveolar hydatis, perish.

HEARTWORMS

Heartworms are thin, extended worms up to 30 cms (12 ins) long, which are difficult to diagnose in cats as the worms are too few to be identified by the antigen-detection test. Symptoms may be loss of energy, loss of appetite, coughing, the development of a potbelly and anaemia. Heartworm infection in cats should be treated very seriously, as it is often fatal.

Heartworms are transmitted by mosquitoes. The mosquito drinks the blood of an infected cat and takes in larvae with the blood. It takes two to three weeks for the larvae to develop to the infective stage within the body of the mosquito. Cats are less frequently infected with heartworms than dogs are. Also, the parasite is more likely to attack the cat's brain or other organs rather than the heart. Cats should be treated at about six weeks of age, and maintained on a prophylactic dose given monthly.

THE FELINE EYE

by Lorraine Waters BvetNed, CertVOphthal, MRCVS

This part of the book aims to provide an owner's guide to feline ophthalmology, the study of eyes, which is an area of increasing concern for cat owners.

Eye diseases in the cat usually result from trauma, infection or neoplasia. Unlike the dog, the cat has few inherited eye conditions. Most of the conditions to be discussed are not amenable to first-aid measures or home remedies. Therefore, if you are at all worried about your cat's eyes, you should seek prompt veterinary attention.

Ocular pain is frequently associated with eye disease and can be recognised in your cat because it will show a combination of the following signs:

blinking, increased tear production, fear of light and rubbing at the eye. Some conditions result in loss of vision; a gradual loss of vision may go unnoticed, as the cat slowly adapts, but a sudden loss produces an obvious change in behaviour. Being blind may not be as bad as it sounds, as cats adapt and cope amazingly well in familiar surroundings.

To examine the eye properly, veterinary surgeons first use a bright light, which allows close examination of the lids, conjunctiva, cornea and iris. Following this, an ophthalmoscope can be used, in a darkened room, to give a magnified view. Then, by using the lenses within the ophthalmoscope, it is possible to focus on the structures further back in the eye, such as the lens, vitreous and retina.

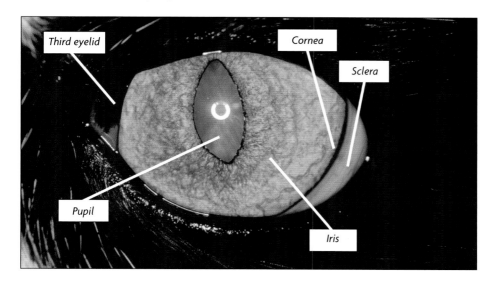

Third eyelid

Cornea

Sclera

Pupil

Iris

The feline fundus, the eye as seen through the veterinary surgeon's ophthalmoscope:

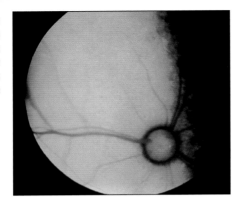

DISEASES OF THE FELINE EYE

GLOBE AND ORBIT

The eye sits in a bony socket in the skull known as the orbit. In short-nosed breeds, the orbit is shallow and the normal-sized eyes bulge forward. This situation can predis-pose a number of problems, such as exposure keratitis, overflow of tears and even prolapse of the globe (eye). Cats can be born with eyes that are too small and sink back into the orbit, to be covered by the third eyelid. This is non-inherited and usually associated with damage to the eye in utero. Abnormal enlargement of the globe may be congenital, buphthalmos, or acquired, hydrophthalmos, and is the end point of glaucoma.

The globe can prolapse from the orbit following head trauma, a common injury for cats involved in road-traffic accidents. A minor prolapse replaced early can result in restoration of normal function. However, there is often stretching of the optic nerve and tearing of the extra-ocular muscles. In these cases, the eye may be permanently damaged and have to be surgically removed. As an emergency measure, applying a moist cloth to the prolapsed eye on the way to the surgery will help preserve it.

Problems behind the eye become evident when they cause the eye to bulge forward along with the third eyelid. These include tooth root abscesses, foreign bodies, tumours and occasionally haemorrhages.

EYELIDS

The eyes of a kitten should open around 10–14 days of age. Once this has occurred, it is possible to see if the lids have been properly formed. Failure of all or part of the eyelids to develop is a rare congen-

EYE DROPS

Topical ointments and drops are often prescribed for the treatment of eye disease. There are a few simple rules to follow when administering them. It is important to clean away discharges before applying treatment. Only give one drop or just a few millilitres of ointment; if you give too much, it will be diluted by increased tear production. Systemic drugs are those given by mouth to achieve higher concentrations at the back of the eye or for diseases which involve other body systems.

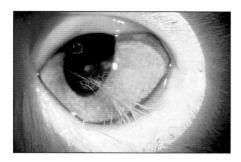

ital problem, known as coloboma. The unprotected cornea, in the affected area, may become damaged and the lid must be surgically restored. Early infection in the eye may delay or prevent the eyelid's opening; the lids can be opened surgically to allow bathing and appropriate medication to be given.

Entropion and ectropion are common conditions in the dog and are related to conformation. Fortunately, these are rare in cats and can be surgically corrected. Entropion secondary to ocular pain may remain once the cause of the pain is removed. Fortunately, these cases will respond to corrective surgery. Extra or abnormally positioned hairs are frequently seen as an inherited problem in dogs, but are rare in cats.

There are several types of tumours that can occur on the eyelids. The most common type is squamous cell carcinoma, more prevalent in white and part-white cats, as ultra-violet light (sunlight) plays a role in causing this condition. Treatment may consist

of cryotherapy, surgical excision or radiation treatment. Early recognition and treatment are essential to prevent destructive local spreading.

Eyelid coloboma is a rare congenital problem in cats.

CONJUNCTIVA

The pink tissue lining the eyelid and covering the third eyelid and front of the sclera is called conjunctiva. Dermoids are elements of skin tissue that arise in abnormal places. Dermoids often, but not invariably, contain hairs and can form on the conjunctiva and/or cornea. Dermoids act as foreign bodies in the eye, causing irritation and pain, and need to be surgically removed.

The most frequently encountered problem with the conjunctiva is conjunctivitis. In cats, the majority of cases are infectious. An eye with conjunctivitis usually looks red and swollen with signs of ocular pain. Discharges may be watery or sticky yellow, indicating bacterial infection.

The most common infectious cause of feline conjunctivitis is feline herpesvirus (FHV). Feline calicivirus (FCV) can also cause

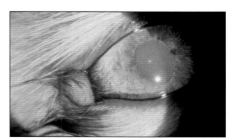

Dermoid in a longhaired cat .

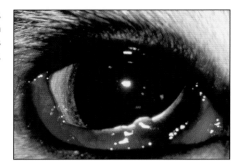

Conjunctivitis, frequently an infectious disease in cats.

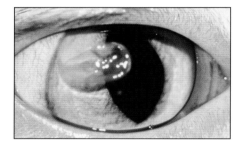

Corneal ulcer stained with fluorescein.

Tear staining is more commonly seen in short-nosed cat breeds.

conjunctivitis and is usually associated with other problems, such as upper respiratory tract signs and mouth ulcers. The bacteria *Chlamydia psittaci* can cause conjunctivitis in individual cats and in multi-cat households. Individual cases respond well to appropriate antibiotic therapy. Chronic and recurrent conjunctivitis in multi-cat situations requires thorough and prolonged treatment, management changes and, where appropriate, vaccination. *Mycoplasma spp.* can cause a less severe conjunctivitis than *Chlamydia spp.* Opportunistic infection can occur following cat-fight wounds, as bacteria are found on cats' teeth and claws.

Non-infectious causes of conjunctivitis include trauma, foreign bodies, allergic disease, tumours and pre-corneal tear film abnormalities. Eosinophilic kerato-conjunctivitis is a disease in which the conjunctiva and cornea are invaded by cells from the immune system, primarily mast cells and eosinophils. These cells are responsible for inflammation and allergic reactions. This tends to occur in young to middle-aged cats and may be seasonal. Treatment usually works well but may be required long-term.

Several forms of neoplasia (cancer) can affect the conjunctiva in cats and can be either primary tumours arising in the conjunctiva or secondary, spreading from elsewhere in the body.

SCLERA
The sclera is the white fibrous coat of the globe. It is partially covered by conjunctiva and protects the more fragile internal structures. Congenital defects of this structure are very rare. Inflammation

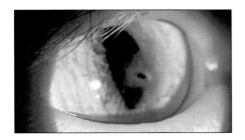

(scleritis and episcleritis) is a problem in dogs and humans but is extremely rare in cats. Feline scleral diseases are usually associated with trauma and cancer.

PRE-CORNEAL TEAR FILM

This forms from tears and moistens, lubricates and helps protect the cornea. Decreased tear production occurs if the tear glands are not working properly and results in a condition called 'dry eye' or keratoconjunctivis sicca (KCS). The cornea becomes dry and roughened, leading to keratitis and ulceration. It can occur following feline herpesvirus (FHV) infection, trauma, facial paralysis and chronic inflammation.

Overproduction of tears can be seen as a result of ocular pain. The naso-lacrimal duct drains the tears; it runs from the inner corner of the eye to just inside the end of the nose. Congenital defects, such as a small duct opening, result in tear overflow and staining around the eye. These usually can be corrected surgically. Acquired blockages may result from chronic conjunctivitis or foreign bodies.

Tear staining is also seen in short-nosed breeds because the duct is tortuous and drainage inadequate. This is also associated with medial lower lid entropion, occluding the duct opening. This anatomical combination is very difficult to improve surgically.

Corneal foreign body.

CORNEA

The cornea is the clear circular area at the front of the eye through which the iris and pupil can be seen. Light passes through and is focused by the cornea, before passing through the lens and hence onto the retina. Congenital defects are rare but include micro- and megalocornea. There is sometimes a transient cloudiness following the kitten's opening of the eyes, but it should disappear by four weeks of age.

One of the most common problems involving the cornea is ulceration, where the top layer of corneal cells (the epithelium) is lost and the nerve endings exposed, resulting in ocular pain. Fluorescein is a special stain that

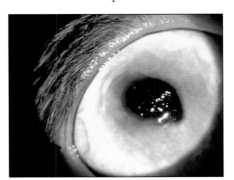

Corneal sequestrum.

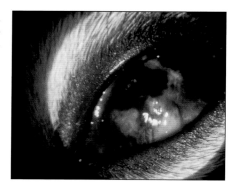

Symblepharon, adhesion of the eyelid to the eyeball.

can be used to reveal ulcers; they show up as a yellow/green patch on the cornea. If your cat has had this performed, you may have noticed the stain appearing at the end of its nose; this is because it drains down the naso-lacrimal duct and demonstrates that it is not blocked.

The most common cause of ulceration is trauma, from fight wounds or foreign bodies. FHV can cause ulceration. There is also a form of ulceration where the epithelium does not stick down again after healing and can easily become detached. This is seen as a breed-related problem in dogs. In cats, it can be seen in older animals or associated with FHV infection, resulting in recurrent ulcer formation.

The cornea is very quick to repair ulcers and, provided that the initial cause is removed, healing should only take a few days. Antibiotics are often applied to the eye while ulcers heal to prevent bacterial infection. Ulcers need

prompt veterinary attention as they can deteriorate rapidly; deep ulcers can lead to rupture of the eye and require urgent surgical repair.

The cornea is a common site for cat-scratch injuries and some may even penetrate the full thickness into the anterior chamber. If these wounds are repaired quickly and appropriate medical therapy is used, vision can usually be preserved. More severe ones may require reconstructive surgery, removal of the lens or even surgical removal of the eye.

Corneal foreign bodies usually result in ocular pain and need to be removed. Non-painful ones also need to be removed as they may penetrate the eye, causing internal problems.

Corneal sequestrum or necrosis is a condition specific to cats. The corneal stroma (middle layer) degenerates, turns brown/black and emerges through the epithelium, causing ulceration and a foreign body reaction with signs of ocular pain. These lesions usually need to be removed surgically because of the discomfort they cause, but a few will slough off naturally. Often a sequestrum will recur in the same eye or occur in the opposite eye at a later date. This condition is most commonly seen in Colourpoint Persians and is thought to have an inherited component. It may be related to their prominent eye position.

Following healing of a corneal

wound, there is usually formation of a scar, which shows up as a white mark, but unless scars are extensive, they do not usually affect vision.

FHV-RELATED EYE DISEASES

A combination of treatments is often required to treat feline herpesvirus (FHV) infection. In acute cases, kittens are often very sick and need supportive treatment and intensive nursing. Systemic and topical antibiotics are used, sometimes in combination with topical antiviral drugs. Cats that develop symblepharon after acute infection may be blinded by the condition and require new reconstructive surgical techniques. The chronic cases can be difficult to diagnose and challenging to treat. Topical antivirals can be used and in non-ulcerated cases combined with corticosteroids. More recent treatments include L-lysine (to inhibit viral replication), Cimetidine and alpha-interferon (to boost the local immune response).

The reason for chronic FHV disease is that individuals become carriers of the virus. When they are stressed, the virus is reactivated and signs of infection and the cat's immune response to it manifest in the eye. This can be a major problem in multi-cat households, with carrier animals infecting kittens and adults alike. In these cases, management changes, including the identification of

carriers, use of early vaccinations and isolation of new arrivals, must be instituted.

AQUEOUS HUMOUR

The aqueous humour is a watery fluid that is responsible for maintaining pressure within the eye. If the drainage angle is blocked and aqueous cannot drain away, pressure within the eye builds up, causing glaucoma. Glaucoma due to a congenitally obstructed drainage system is an inherited problem in many breeds of dog but is rare in the cat. When glaucoma does occur in cats, it is usually acquired, with drainage blocked by inflammatory or neoplastic cells.

Anterior uveitis can result in white blood cells in the anterior chamber, which gives it a cloudy look known as aqueous flare. Infection following penetrating wounds can result in pus accumulating in the chamber, known as hypopyon. Trauma to the eye and intra-ocular tumours may lead to bleeding into the anterior chamber (space behind the cornea and in front of the iris), known as

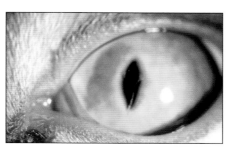

Herpesvirus ulcer.

hyphaema. This blood usually forms a clot and is absorbed. Foreign bodies also occasionally can be seen in the anterior chamber.

IRIS AND CILIARY BODY
The iris and ciliary body are muscular and vascular structures that lie behind the cornea and in front of the lens. The iris is pigmented and gives the cat's eye its colour. Congenital defects are rare, but occasionally cats are born with pieces of the iris missing. Changes in iris colour can occur for a number of reasons; as young cats mature, their iris colour may deepen. Inflammation results in reddening of the iris, due to an increase in blood vessel formation and engorgement, and is known as rubeosis iridis. Following inflammation, the iris can remain permanently dark. As cats age, they can develop a condition called melanosis. This is usually but not always a diffuse change, occurring slowly in both eyes. It must be monitored and differentiated from

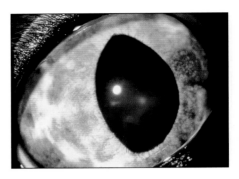

iris melanoma. Melanoma is a tumour of the pigment cells that can result in either diffuse or nodular discoloration of the iris. It usually progresses quickly and only in one eye. This type of neoplasia has a potential to spread outside the eye and is usually treated by surgically removing the affected eye.

A difference in colour between the two irises is known as heterochromia iridis and can occur naturally in white or poorly pigmented breeds, usually associated with congenital deafness. In other cats, it usually indicates a problem in one eye or the other.

The ciliary body and iris are known as the anterior uvea, while the choroid (the vascular layer that lies between the retina and the sclera and provides a blood supply to the retina) is the posterior uvea. Uveitis is an inflammation of the uvea. It may involve both the anterior and posterior uvea and has many causes in the cat. The main infectious causes are feline immunodeficiency virus (FIV),

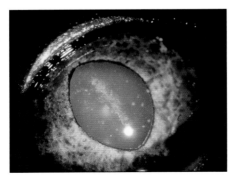

Iris melanoma, exhibited as a tumour of pigment cells that results in discoloration of the iris.

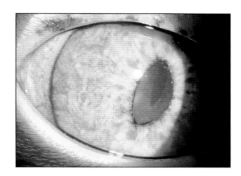

feline leukaemia virus (FeLV), feline infectious peritonitis (FIP) and toxoplasmosis. Tuberculosis has been reported in cats as a cause of uveitis and, in sub-tropical and tropical countries, fungal infection can be a significant cause. The signs of uveitis for all of these diseases are very similar and may include a constricted pupil, rubeosis iridis, aqueous flare, poor vision and ocular pain. It can be difficult to determine the cause in some cases despite thorough investigation. Even if the primary viral infection cannot be cured, cats with uveitis can be treated sympto-matically to ease discomfort and maintain vision. Long-term uveitis can lead to cataract formation, lens luxation and glaucoma. Non-infectious causes of uveitis include trauma and neoplasia.

Atrophy of the iris may occur as a result of ageing or following inflammation. Cysts of the iris are sometimes seen and look like tiny black balloons. They form on the back of the iris but can detach and float through the pupil to rest in front. They are not neoplastic and do not usually need to be removed.

Lens

The lens is the clear disc-shaped structure suspended behind the iris, responsible for focusing light onto the retina. A cataract, or opacity of the lens and/or its capsule, is a disorder of the lens. Many forms of hereditary cataracts are seen in dogs but not in cats. Congenital cataracts are occasion-ally found as a non-inherited problem. Most of the cataracts seen in cats are formed secondary to lens damage, e.g. blunt trauma, penetrating wounds, chronic anterior uveitis and lens luxation. If cataracts involve the whole lens, light will not be able to get through to the retina and the eye will be rendered blind. If appropriate, cataracts can be surgically removed.

If the lens's suspensory fibres weaken or break, it will become dislocated and can fall either into the back or front of the eye. This is a common breed-related problem in terrier dogs and is occasionally seen in cats, usually as a result of

Uveitis, inflamma-tion of the iris, ciliary body and choroid.

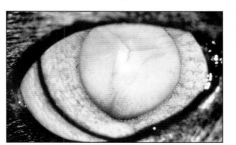

Cataract developed from long-term uveitis.

trauma, ageing or cataract. The lens usually is surgically removed to prevent it from blocking the pupil, which can lead to glaucoma.

The lens condenses with age, giving it a grey appearance, known as senile sclerosis. This is not a true cataract, as light can still pass through to the back of the eye and vision is not impaired.

One rare but important condition of the lens in the cat is post-traumatic sarcoma. If the lens is damaged by trauma, it can become neoplastic and rapidly fill the eye with tumours. Appropriate treatment at the time of the initial injury should prevent this, but when it does occur, surgical removal of the eye is recommended.

VITREOUS HUMOUR

The vitreous humour is a jelly-like substance that fills the space between the back of the lens and the front of the retina. Like the aqueous humour, the vitreous can be infiltrated with haemorrhage and inflammatory cells. Foreign bodies can occasionally be found in the vitreous. Inflammation of the vitreous, known as hyalitis, can be seen as part of generalised uveitis.

The vitreous humour degenerates with age, giving a cloudy appearance to the back of the eye, but this does not usually affect vision to any great extent.

THINGS TO LOOK OUT FOR
A change in appearance of the eye
• Redness
• Cloudiness
• Change in iris colour
Increase in discharges
• Watery
Sticky mucoid
• Yellow
• Bloody
Blinking, squinting and head shyness
Aversion to light
Rubbing at the eye
Loss of vision
Protrusion of the eye
Loss of facial symmetry

RETINA

The retina, at the back of the eye, is where the visual image is formed. Congenital retinal problems are rare in cats, but colobomas (defects or holes) can occasionally be seen in the optic disc (the point at which nerves converge to leave the eye as the optic nerve). Inflammation of the retina usually occurs together with inflammation of the choroid and is called chorioretinitis or posterior uveitis. The causes are the same as those for anterior uveitis. Inflammation can lead to retinal detachment, haemorrhage, degeneration and scarring of the retina. It can be difficult to diagnose the cause of posterior uveitis; thus, symptomatic treatment is generally given to

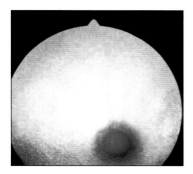

maintain vision.

The retina may also degenerate as a result of non-inflammatory processes. An inherited form of retinal degeneration has been described in the Abyssinian and Siamese breeds. Deficiency in dietary taurine (an amino acid) causes retinal degeneration. Fortunately, this is now rare as many commercial cat foods are supplemented with this compound. It may, however, still be a problem with some home-prepared diets.

Hypertension is a common cause of retinal disease in elderly cats. It may be primary, essential hypertension or secondary to other diseases, such as kidney disease, hyperthyroidism and diabetes. Hypertension causes changes in the retinal arteries, retinal and vitreal haemorrhages, retinal detachment and hyphaema. Early recognition and treatment are essential to prevent permanent ocular damage and damage to other organs, such as the kidney, heart and brain.

Retinal detachment causes blindness and may result from hypertension, inflammation and neoplasia. If the retina does not reattach in 24–48 hours, there will be permanent vision loss. Symptomatic treatment is often given to reattach the retina, but it is also important to treat the underlying cause.

Retinal haemorrhages can occur as a result of hypertension, inflammation and trauma. They can cause temporary loss of vision but will often be resorbed. Once again, it is important to find the underlying cause and treat it accordingly without delay.

Finally, if in any doubt regarding the condition of your cat's eyes, it is always worthwhile consulting your veterinary surgeon. Even if you consider the condition minor, it may not remain so!

Advanced retinal degeneration.

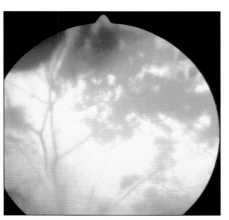

Retinal haemorrhages as a result of hypertension.

The author is grateful to the Animal Health Trust (England) for the illustrations used in the eye-health section.

USEFUL ADDRESSES

GREAT BRITAIN
The Governing Council of the Cat Fancy (GCCF)
4-6 Penel Orlieu, Bridgwater, Somerset, TA6 3PG
Email: GCCF_CATS@compuserve.com Fax: 01278 446627 Tel: 01278 427575

The Cat Association of Britain
Mill House, Letcombe Regis, Oxon OX12 9JD   Tel: 01235 766543

EUROPE
Federation Internationale Feline (FIFe)
Gen. Sec: Ms Penelope Bydlinski
Little Dene, Lenham Heath, Maidstone, Kent ME17 2BS, GB
Email: penbyd@compuserve.com   Fax: 1622 850193 Tel: 1622 850908

World Cat Federation
Hubertsrabe 280, D-45307, Essen, Germany
Email: wcf@nrw-online.de   Fax: 201-552747 Tel: 201-555724

AUSTRALIA
The Australian Cat Federation, Inc.
PO Box 3305, Port Adelaide, SA 5015
Email: acf@catlover.com   Fax: 08 8242 2767 Tel: 08 8449 5880

CANADA
Canadian Cat Association
220 Advance Boulevard, Suite 101, Brampton, Ontario L6T 4J5
Email: office@cca-afc.com   Fax: 99050 459-4023 Tel: 99060 459-1481

SOUTH AFRICA
Cat Federation of Southern Africa
PO Box 25, Bromhof 2154, Gauteng Province, Republic of South Africa

USA
American Cat Association
8101 Katherine Avenue, Panorama City, CA 91402
Fax: (818) 781-5340 Tel: (818) 781-5656

American Cat Fanciers Association
PO Box 203, Point Lookout, MO 65726
Email: info@acfacat.com   Fax: (417) 334-5540 Tel: (417) 334-5430

Cat Fanciers Association, Inc.
PO Box 1005, Manasquan, NJ 08736-0805
Email: cfa@cfainc.org   Fax: (732) 528-7391 Tel: (732) 528-9797

Cat Fanciers Federation
PO Box 661, Gratis, OH 45330
Email: Lalbert933@aol.com Fax: (937) 787-4290 Tel: (937) 787-9009

The International Cat Association
PO Box 2684, Harlingen, TX 78551
Email: ticaeo@xanadu2.net Tel: (956) 428-8046